GOD, YOU ARE INCREDIBLE!

Merle Alexander

Ro 8:28

TRUE STORIES
FROM PEOPLE
WHO HAVE
ENCOUNTERED OUR
INCREDIBLE GOD

God,
You are Incredible!

MERLE L. ALEXANDER

MAJESTY PUBLICATIONS
LAGUNA NIGUEL, CALIFORNIA

DEDICATION

To all earnest seekers
after the living God,
this book is lovingly dedicated.

ACKNOWLEDGMENTS

I AM DEEPLY INDEBTED to a number of people who helped give form to an idea, so this book could come to life.

Dear friends and associates, you who opened your hearts and shared from their deepest depths so others could come to know our incredible God, what can I say? Thank you seems so inadequate, but until something better comes along, it will have to do.

Richard C. Hjelte, editor and trusted friend who carefully and prayerfully prepared the manuscript for publication, you are priceless! Thank you.

Ruby Norton, precious confidante, except for your encouragement and practical support, this venture would have remained a dream. May God richly reward you!

Last, but by no means least, dear family, thank you for keeping me going through the dry spells. You are what every writer needs.

CONTENTS

INTRODUCTION

*T*HERE ARE THOSE AMONG US, who for the past two decades, or longer, have made a concerted effort to deny America's roots-in-God and to wipe all knowledge of God from the public consciousness. They have been alarmingly successful. Under the guise of separating church and state they have trampled on the basic rights of Christians guaranteed by the constitution and, in many ways, persecuted Christians in the country their forefathers founded to escape such persecution.

Now that we are reaping the bitter harvest of such activity, people are beginning to ask, "What went wrong?" A few are asking "Where is God in all of this?" Interestingly enough, these are the very ones who were asserting, "There is no God," only a short time ago.

This attitude reminds me of a story I heard a long time ago and still remember. It describes the situation so very well.

A husband and wife decided to celebrate their silver wedding anniversary by going back to some of their favorite haunts of courtship days.

"Everything looks pretty much the same, don't you think?" asked the husband. "Yes," the wife replied as she was thrown hard against the passenger's door as her husband braked for a deer that darted across the road. "Everything is the same outside, but inside things have changed!" "How is that?" her husband answered. "Oh, don't you remember how we used to sit so close together that we were like one person instead of two? But now we have the whole seat between us and I could have been thrown out if the door had popped open just then." The husband looked a bit bewildered and then said, "But Honey! *I* haven't moved."

Something like that has happened in our country. When we no longer had to spend every ounce of our energies on mere survival, we "inched" away from God until it seemed He no longer existed.

Now as we cry, "Where is God in all of this?" He is saying, "*I* haven't moved." And so He hasn't. God is where He has always been...in the driver's seat! We can sit as close to Him as we want, or move as far away as we can. We can even hurl ourselves out the door, but He isn't moving.

How do I know this is true? For one thing, we still are "one nation under God." I also have the witness of God's moving in my own life and the witness of others who have shared their stories with me.

As I have gone about the country ministering in retreats, camps, seminars and workshops, I have collected hundreds of testimonies of God's fantastic intervention when all seemed lost.

Some of these people have consented to have their stories published that others might benefit from their experiences. They are very private people and I have agreed to identify them by their initials only. In one or two cases, even these have been changed, but all the stories are true.

Of course, there are stories drawn from my own experience. These stories are signed, M.L.A.

As I have worked with the various testimonies over the past several months, I have heard myself saying, "God! You are incredible!" It seemed a fitting title for the book. It's all about God...

God providing...God healing...God rescuing...God bringing order out of chaos.

When we lose contact with Him, he will allow such experiences as are necessary to bring us back again. He knows there is no other safe road that will take us home and no other "designated driver" to see that we get there.

If the people who have always known this and stayed close to their Lord through every circumstance made as good a news copy as those with a different agenda, we would recognize ourselves for who we are...people after God's own heart. May this sharing of testimonies bring us that recognition.

The stories have been grouped into categories according to the relationship shown between God (whose name is Jehovah) and mankind. For example, in the Old Testament, the name Jehovah-jireh means "God provides." Similarly, God demonstrates his kindness toward us through the following: Jehovah-shammah (God is ever present), Jehovah-nissi (God is my banner), Jehovah-shalom (God is our peace), etc.

Of course with some stories, God shows more than one aspect of His character, for nothing with God is ever cut-and-dried. He is always present in all His ways, but we perceive Him in relation to our specific needs.

There will also be variations in the way certain names are spelled and pronounced, depending on the translation being used, but the meanings are the same.

God is! God moves! God works! God is Alpha and Omega, the beginning and the end. Of that there is no doubt!

"Give thanks to the Lord, proclaim his greatness, tell the nations what he has done. Sing praise to the Lord, tell the wonderful things he has done. Be glad that we belong to him, let all who worship him rejoice. Go to the Lord for help and worship him continually. You descendants of Abraham, his servant, you descendants of Jacob, the man he chose, remember the miracles that God performed and the judgments that he gave. The Lord is our God, his commandments are for all the world. He will keep his covenant forever, his promises for a thousand generations." Psalm 105:1-8 Good News Bible

It is by obeying this command that we "pay our dues" to this generation. It is in that spirit, these stories are offered.

JEHOVAH JIREH

Circuit Rider

WHEN I WAS GROWING UP, the stories my mother told us that intrigued me most, concerned her maternal great grandfather, Stephen Fairchild, one of the last of the old "Circuit Riders," who brought the gospel to the unsettled West on horseback. He was said to be a "legend in his own time," because of his monumental faith.

Although his time in history (the 1840's and 50's), was well after John Wesley's time, the same fire burned in his heart, that had burned in the heart of his "idol." Wesley's command, "Give them Christ," was a clarion call to Stephen Fairchild, who rode the same trails blazed by the earlier "Circuit Riders," with a zeal as great as their own.

Mother's mother, was raised in the Fairchild home, and was a participant in the "mighty acts of God" that took place there. She passed the stories on to her children, and Mother passed them to us.

Fairchild's wife, Mary Elizabeth, like most of the women of her day who were brave enough to marry preachers, saw herself as part and parcel of her husband's ministry. His calling was to preach. Her calling was to see that he did. To this end, she must release him from all household responsibilities. She must be able to function as well when he was gone, as when he was home. Since he covered his circuit four times a year, and each trip took a month, this was a tall order.

Mary Elizabeth took as her role model, the description of a "virtuous woman," found in the book of Proverbs, 31: 10-31, and she lived it to the letter. Her price was, indeed, "far above rubies," and "the heart of her husband, did safely trust in her."

It is highly doubtful that Stephen Fairchild would have been "a legend in his own time," without her faithful support.

Stephen Fairchild planted churches across the territory that would become Nebraska and Kansas, and with every church, a school. Like Wesley, he knew the futility of bringing illiterate people to Christ and leaving them there. They must be able to read the Bible and develop other skills for living.

Mary Elizabeth was a professional dressmaker, (one of the best), and with her earnings; provided for her household and her husband's schools.

Life was hard and challenging, but for them, very rewarding. God gave them a deep love for the "plains people," both the immigrant settlers and the natives that were called Indians in their day. They were loved in return and would have been worshipped if they had allowed it. They didn't.

Their one sorrow was for their baby daughter who was never very strong.

Little Mary lived on miracles throughout her sickly childhood, but seemed to grow stronger as she developed into a lovely young woman. Still, her parents weren't too thrilled when she fell in love with a man "a bit older" than herself and married at nineteen.

Her husband, Tom, was suffering from "gold fever" and was determined to take his bride to the "gold fields" of California. Before they could leave, however, Mary was in "a delicate condition," so her husband went on without her, promising to send for her and the baby when he was "established."

Due to his much moving, it was nearly two years before word reached him that Mary had died in childbirth and the Fairchilds were raising his baby daughter.

Oh well! It was too late to be a family man now. He might as well push on.

Mary's baby seemed to inherit her mother's weakness, whatever it was. It would be many years before anybody would know it was a congenital heart defect.

Trying to raise a baby without a mother was the most challenging task the Fairchilds ever faced. Baby cried incessantly because she was hungry. Nothing they tried to feed her agreed with her...not boiled cow's milk...not goat's milk...not anything except barley water and molasses. She couldn't take enough of this to thrive. She lost ground and her anxious grandparents gave her back to God.

"Perhaps it is best if the little thing goes to her mother," Mary Elizabeth said one day. Her husband nodded. They couldn't have guessed at the time that God had a different idea and that help was on the way. They almost didn't recognize it when it came.

How often do we stumble over God's answers because we would have never thought of such a thing? Praise God His ways are not our ways, nor His thoughts our thoughts!

Armeda

THE YOUNG INDIAN GIRL STAGGERED and nearly fell on the hot dusty plain. How long had she been following the wagon tracks she had been told led to the white man's mission? She couldn't remember. Time had lost all significance. She cooled her hot face with the last drops of water in her canteen and shifted the weight of the bundle she carried in her hand. Maybe she should set it down and leave it. She probably wouldn't reach the mission anyway, so the beads and trinkets she hoped to barter for room and board wouldn't be needed. She had learned in the mission school that one, Jesus, would take her to His home when she died. Maybe that was now.

Weak from recent birthing and breasts heavy with milk made her so miserable, she no longer cared to live. Where was Jesus? She was ready.

Five days previous, the girl had given birth to a baby boy fathered by a white man. The baby died. The girl was cast out of her tribe. She knew the taboo!

The girl was past thinking now. She didn't hear the hoof beats behind her, or feel the strong but gentle arms that lifted her onto a horse. Stephen Fairchild thanked God the mission was so close. This poor child couldn't have lasted much longer.

Mary Elizabeth helped her husband bring the still form into the house. Only little moans told them she was still alive. Tenderly, Mary Elizabeth bathed her and slipped one of her own night dresses on her; Stephen laid her on the little day bed in the corner of the multi-purpose room where they lived, and took turns with his wife, squeezing drops of cool water into the parched mouth, from a soft cloth.

The girl revived in about an hour and took little sips of

chicken broth they warmed for her. Then, she dozed again. The anxiety was gone. This dear little one of God's family was on her way to recovery.

The Fairchilds talked in low tones, as they pondered where their guest had come from and how long would it be before someone who knew her would show up.

It was Baby's cries that finally called to the sleeping girl. She sat bolt upright and commanded, "Bring me the baby!"

Mary Elizabeth was startled by this sudden change in the girl. "Where did you learn to speak English?" she asked. "In your mission school," she answered, looking at Stephen. "I know you. You are the missionary and I am Armeda." She seemed to think this would identify her to Stephen. It didn't. He only visited the schools occasionally and was vaguely aware of the shy Indian children who came and went.

Again Armeda commanded, "Bring me the baby. See I have milk and no baby. He died when he was born."

Without another moment's hesitation, Baby was put to Armeda's breast where she started to nurse as though she had been doing it since she was born.

"It's a miracle!" said Stephen as he sank to his knees in worship.

It was a day of new beginnings at the mission. Baby grew healthy and strong on Armeda's tender care and gentle nursing. Mary Elizabeth went about singing again. She had a new daughter to love who loved her in return. She made Armeda new dresses and bonnets and taught her to wind her dark braids about her head, white woman style.

Armeda made herself useful about the place, never waiting to be asked to help with the chores. She was also an eager learner and literally soaked up the Bible lessons that were part of daily life. She loved the hymns they sang and soon added her flute-like voice to the morning and evening worship.

Why then, was Stephen unable to enter into the joy of his own household? Why did he feel like the odd man out? Even as he asked, he knew. Armeda! Try as he would not to resent the bonding of Armeda and Baby he couldn't, He knew his feelings were unreasonable, but they were there just the same.

What hurt most of all, was seeing Mary Elizabeth and Armeda together. Had his wife forgotten their daughter? It was to be expected that a nursing baby would bond to the one who fed her, but for his wife, there was no excuse. How could she put this "wild little thing of the prairie," in their lovely child's place? Or had she?

Because Stephen wouldn't think of admitting his feelings to anybody, he bore his cross alone. For the first time in his life, he was forced to face the darkness of his own heart. Darkness, where he supposed no darkness existed. Wasn't he a man of light?

Mary Elizabeth was happy to see him take off to visit his churches. She didn't know what was bothering him, but something certainly was. Maybe the long winter had depressed him. Getting out in the spring sunshine was probably what he needed.

So Stephen Fairchild rode across the prairie, weeping his heart out as he swayed to the rhythm of the horse's movements and owned his "demons" within. He had supposed himself immune to the vices of other men. It was a blow to find out, he wasn't.

Selfishness, arrogance, prejudice and pride, that he hated so much in others and preached so vehemently against, lurked in the depths of his heart also.

How he had loved the simple "Plains People," but not enough to make one a member of the family. He wanted Armeda to disappear, now that Baby was weaned. Wasn't that "using" people?

22

And Stephen had another problem. Was he in some way betraying his daughter? Was it superstitious to think she might have sent Armeda to save her starving baby?

So he learned what many other missionaries have learned in other settings.

It is one thing to go to a "heathen land," and "*Give them Christ* " and quite another to live in that land and *be* Christ, insofar as humanly possible. He realized that until he could do exactly that, his offering to His Maker was incomplete.

It wasn't easy, but there came a time when this man of God was able to offer a complete gift. He would adopt Armeda, give her his name and set her in his heart beside his own lovely daughter. The ecstasy that followed that decision made all the pain and struggle worthwhile.

When he told his wife about it after he got home, she got busy planning a celebration dinner for when they told her.

Sometime in the night, before the big day, Stephen dreamed of hearing a horse neighing nearby, but didn't come fully awake. In the morning, he was awakened by Baby's shrieks. She had her feet tangled in her long nightgown as she tried to climb out of her crib.

Armeda was nowhere to be seen.

In the middle of the big round dining table stood an exquisitely beaded pair of white buckskin booties, just fitting Baby's dainty feet. All the "white woman's" clothes were left hanging in the closet and the Indian outfit, Armeda had arrived in was gone.

Stephen remembering his dream of the night went to check the barn and his worst fear was confirmed.

His very best horse that had carried him for miles and seemed almost human, was gone. Though inquiry was made far and near, neither the girl nor the horse was ever seen nor heard from again. It was as though neither had ever existed.

One wag suggested that perhaps Armeda wasn't mortal, but an angel sent in time of need.

"Angels don't steal horses," Stephen had answered tersely. "Or make beaded moccasins," his wife countered. There the matter rested forever.

Baby adjusted to the loss of Armeda more quickly than anyone thought she would. In some uncanny way, she seemed to realize, life had taken a different turn. She accepted the attentions of her grandparents in a way she hadn't before. Happiness reigned once more.

The next big event at the mission was the annual visit of the Superintendent to check on the work of the missionaries. Each little church and school would be inspected and the "class meeting" leaders examined in their faith, doctrine and ability to lead. To Stephen Fairchild, it was equivalent to standing before God and accounting for his stewardship. He was always glad when it was over and his work accepted.

This was also the time when delayed rites and ceremonies of the church were celebrated. Baptisms, confirmations, the blessing of marriages and memorial services all waited for the Superintendent. This year, Baby would be christened and receive a real name.

The little chapel at the mission was decorated with such wild flowers as were in bloom, making a lovely setting for the ceremony.

Baby, dressed in the delicate little christening dress her mother had made before she was born, and on her feet the little buckskin beaded booties, was carried to the front by her grandfather and accompanied by her grandmother.

"What is the child to be named" asked the Superintendent.

"Mary Armeda," Grandpa answered firmly as Grandmother smiled her approval.

Mary Armeda treasured her lovely name as long as she lived

and would love to have been called by it, but she never was. Just plain, simple, Molly was all she ever got. Molly was my maternal grandmother.

I never knew her. She died before I was born, but when I played house and pretended to go visit her, I called her Mary Armeda. I think she smiled.

—M.L.A

In Grandfather's House

MOLLY'S CHILDHOOD WAS AS NEARLY PERFECT as any childhood could be. The only treasure of doting grandparents though she was, they never spoiled her. She learned early the value of work and did her share with a willing heart. She inherited her grandmother's unique ability with a needle and began doing the "plain sewing" on Mary Elizabeth's creations at a young age. From there, she moved on, and in time, was every bit as accomplished as her grandmother.

She absorbed her grandfather's Christian teachings and made them her own. She appreciated most of all his transparency before God and man. It was he who told her about her own mother and about Armeda who had saved her. He also told her of his heart struggles to overcome his prejudice and pride. For that she truly respected him.

"You are in trouble," he told her, "when you start believing the myths people build up around you. Only the truly humble, can be truly useful."

Molly did not forget. The example of a truly humble and truly useful servant of God was ever before her.

Of all the stories Molly told her daughters about life in

Grandfather's house, there was one they asked for again and again, and we asked our mother for it repeatedly.

It concerned a year when a late freeze delayed the spring planting. Then a late summer "dry spell" with accompanying hot winds, parched the corn in the fields and withered almost everything else on the vine. As a final insult, "a great cloud of grasshoppers" came through and consumed what was left.

That was a tough winter for the settlers. Supplies ran low and cows went dry for lack of feed. Chickens went into a moult and ended up on dinner plates. Even wild game grew scarce.

Before spring, people were eating their meager suppers early in the evening and going to bed immediately thereafter, to save fuel.

Desperate folk turned to the missionary who shared until he was finally staring at the bottom of his own meal barrel.

He went on a "protracted fast," and his wife soon joined him. The last handfuls of corn meal and drops of molasses must be saved for little Molly. The Bible became her grandparent's "meat."

Molly remembered when she ate her last bowl of corn meal mush. She hadn't been told it was the last, she just knew.

Grandpa sat in his rocking chair with an open Bible on his lap, his eyes closed and his head tilted back.

Grandma tried in vain to keep her mind on a bit of sewing. At last she asked, "Has God spoken?"

"Just now!" he shouted. "Put on your best tablecloth and set out the wedding china!"

Fearfully, she obeyed. Had the strain been too much for her husband? Had it "quite addled" his brain?

"Stay near the door," he whispered to Molly, "and listen for the wagons."

The wagons weren't long in coming. First one, then two, then the wagons filled the yard.

"Surprise! Surprise!" shouted the first people through the door. "It's a pound party!"

Pound parties were common in those days before welfare and food banks. It was the way neighbors helped each other. They would go to their cupboards and weigh out a pound of something ...flour, corn meal, coffee, beans, whatever they could spare. Then they would put the "pounds" together and take it to the one who needed it, always bringing "a dish to pass" so they could have a party.

This was the kind of party brought to Grandpa and Grandma Fairchild that night so long ago. One woman seeing the table spread so elegantly, said, "Ohhhhh! This was supposed to be a surprise. Who told you?"

Stephen Fairchild lifted his eyes toward the ceiling and said simply, "Father did!"

The shared feast ended in a "Praise-Fest," in honor of the One who always provides for His children.

When the last wagon left, Molly helped her grandparents put the "pounds" in the pantry. Where had such abundance come from when nobody had anything to speak of? They hoped they weren't taking bread out of other mouths. They weren't.

The answer came the next day. Three families who had been "laying by" supplies for a trip to California in the spring, suddenly decided to wait another year to go. The supplies were shared and probably saved the settlement from starvation.

When had such a decision been made and why? Was the Fairchilds' "protracted fast" in any way responsible? Molly always thought so.

Later, when she was reading the Bible, words seemed to rise off the printed page and hang before her startled eyes.

"...and when Jacob saw the wagons which Joseph had sent, his spirit revived and he said" 'It is enough, Joseph, my son is alive.' (Gen. 45:27-28)

That had been her experience! Until that night when the food was gone, "faith" had been a "shadowy something" Molly's grandparents had. But when she saw the wagons, "faith" materialized into corn and beans, sugar and flour, molasses, tea and coffee. Her spirit did revive as she realized her "Joseph," (named Jesus) was alive and would not let his children starve.

Molly called for the wagons herself, many times as she grew up. More often than not, they came. But there were a few that didn't.

No wagon ever brought Armeda. Every time she was told the story, she longed for that girl who had saved her life. Perhaps it was the longing of a child for her mother.

She learned early not to say anything about her father. Grandpa and Grandma were apparently still angry with him, but sometimes Molly pretended a wagon would bring him, and she secretly asked for one.

In due time Molly grew up and married. She had four daughters. My mother was the third. She was also the only robust one...the only one to live to old age. The tendencies to heart defects were a fact of life in that family. Nevertheless, they all experienced the goodness of the God who provides.

Molly's Wagon

GRANDPA AND GRANDMA FAIRCHILD had been dead a few years. Molly was grown and raising her own family, but her grandparents were never far from her thoughts. Their influence on her life could be seen in everything she did. She never forgot the wagons of the settlers who brought a "pound party" when there was no food. She believed with all her heart, that what

God had done once, He could and would do again.

There came a year somewhat like the one she had experienced as a child. Somewhat...but not one and the same. Actually, it was the reverse of that year. Instead of drought and grasshoppers, conditions had been ideal. Everybody had a bumper crop of everything.

The big surpluses caused prices to "bottom out." Hogs sold for a cent a pound on the hoof. Cattle not much better. Corn couldn't be given away. Farmers were burning it for fuel.

One night when it was bitter cold, Molly's husband, Henry, went over to see his brother who lived a mile away. The children thought he was going to ask Uncle Dick for a loan, but Molly knew better. Henry "drank some" when he was upset and he usually drank with Uncle Dick. To quiet her worries, she sang to her daughters and told them stories of her life at the mission with her grandparents. Of course the story of the "wagons" was told once more.

"Have you sent for Grandfather's wagons?" one of the children asked. "Yes," she had replied, "but they are my wagons now."

No sooner were the words out of her mouth, but there came a knock at the door. Molly answered in fear and trembling, thinking Uncle Dick was bringing Henry home. But, to her relief, a well-dressed man stood on the doorstep and she invited him in.

"I wonder if you could help me," he said as he sat down at the table and accepted a cup of coffee. "I'm looking for a woman named Molly who was raised by her grandparents, Stephen and Mary Fairchild."

It took a moment or two for Molly to recover from the shock, then she answered, "I'm Molly and my grandparents raised me. My mother died when I was born."

"And your father?" queried the stranger. "He went west," Molly answered. "He hasn't been heard from since. Grandpa and

Grandma were never certain he got the message about my mother and me."

"He got the message Molly; I am your father. I have been trying to find you for a very long time."

"How long?" Molly asked skeptically.

"I admit I waited until I heard the Fairchilds were both dead. I don't think they liked me very well."

After introductions, the girls were put to bed, while Molly and "Grandpa Tom" sat up most of the night talking.

The next day the girls were delighted to learn Grandpa Tom had driven Molly's wagon right up to the door. He brought a bag of gold coins he had been saving for her for a long time.

"I promised your mother I would send for her when I struck gold," he explained. "Well...I didn't strike gold but I did well trapping. By the time I could have sent for the two of you, she was dead. How could I raise a baby alone? I kept pushing on, doing all kinds of things that brought in money. I always put a little aside for my little Molly. I would take it to her...someday."

My mother never knew how much money was in that bag but she did know it pulled them out of a deep hole. Grandpa Tom never lost track of them again and it was not the last money he ever brought.

To Molly, finding her father was the ultimate gift sent by her heavenly Father. The money always came in handy, but it was second to having "the other half of the loaf" that had been missing in her life.

Grossmamma

NOT ALL OF MOTHER'S SPIRITUAL HERITAGE came from her mother, Molly and Molly's grandparents. When Molly's health began to fail and she needed help in running her household, Mother's paternal grandmother (called Grossmamma), came to live with them.

Mother described her as being the very opposite of the gentle, vulnerable Fairchilds, who "walked softly before the Lord," all the days of their lives, lest they offend Him in some unintentional way.

Grossmamma had no such worries. She walked firmly and determinedly in the footsteps of "The Great Reformer," which meant, among other things, that she was always right.

She knew God was watching every minute, trying to catch His children breaking some of His many rules, or enjoying themselves too much. She did neither. God, Himself, could ask no more.

She had come from Germany as a girl of twenty, in search of the "American Dream." She was wise enough to know that a dream can only take shape if the dreamer is willing to put forth the effort to shape it. She would shape hers no matter what it took. No work was too menial or too hard.

She soon met a young man, George Friederich, who was from her part of Germany. He shared her dreams and ideals. They fell in love, married, and brought six children into the world. Life was challenging and happy. They taught their children to work hard and to dream.

George, a man of deep convictions, believed freedom was the birthright of all and seemed driven to help secure it for all.

It was no surprise then, that he volunteered in the Union

Army at the outset of the Civil War. His wife did not try to dissuade him. If he *must* go, so be it!

George was killed in that war and his wife bore her lot dry eyed and with a stiff spine. She would not dishonor her husband's sacrifice for freedom by whining. She would never remarry. She had given George all the love she had to give. Theirs was a young love that never grew old and never died.

It wasn't easy to raise such a large family all alone, but life had never been easy for this lady. I do believe she was the original "possibility thinker," from which all others have been fashioned. When others talked problems, she talked solutions. When others moaned over closed doors, she looked for open windows. She taught her children to do likewise.

Her tiny widow's pension wasn't enough to live on, but it was enough to secure a bank loan. Nobody ever knew how many times it was so used.

When crops were small and prices down, she turned to the one thing she could always depend on. Her hair!

As a young girl in Germany, she had discovered the wig makers of France who paid premium prices for the right kind of hair. She had it! It was so heavy and grew so fast it had to be thinned regularly to prevent headaches. So...why waste it? Why not harvest it? In this way she saved the money for passage to America.

Now, in her mature years, and faced with the needs of a growing family, Grossmamma turned once more to harvesting her hair. That hair remained abundant into her eighties and never turned gray! Oh what God will do for a "possibility thinker."

After her family was grown, Grossmamma finally became uncomfortable living alone. She "boarded around" among her children and was a Godsend everywhere she went. She insisted upon giving the family she was with, her monthly pension and it took "some doing" to find ways to give it back to her so she wouldn't catch on.

At one point in her mid-nineties, God gave her a trip to Paradise. She was never sure if she dreamed it or if she had really made a round trip, but it did not matter. She told of the most beautiful garden she could ever imagine. Flowers, trees, shrubs, the like of which she didn't know existed, and "unbelievable" birds were everywhere. There was a gate to an "inner garden" that looked so enticing she wanted to see what was beyond, but when she went to open the gate, a very gentle voice said, "Not now Amelia, but soon."

After that, Mother said Grossmamma softened into the kind of person she was always meant to be. She still worked at her outdoor chores and kept all the rules she was supposed to, but the "grimness" was gone.

On her last day on earth, Grossmamma rose at her usual five o'clock, went out and gathered the eggs and cleaned the chicken house. After breakfast she put a chicken on to cook and said she was going to lie down for a little bit but to call her when it was time to put in the dumplings.

Her daughter, Jetta, with whom she was living at the time, promised to call her, but grew uneasy almost immediately. It wasn't like her mother to lie down in the day time. Only lazy people did that!

When Jetta checked, she saw right away that her mother was gone. With a smile on her face, that looked amazingly young, Amelia Friederich had stepped out of the dream of this life, and into the reality of eternal life, as easily as she would have gone to the field on a sunny day.

She was one hundred years old, minus eight days.

—M.L.A.

Grossmamma's Child

AFTER LISTENING CAREFULLY TO MOTHER'S STORIES about her paternal grandmother, and from the tales my father told about that austere lady, I have come to the conclusion that my mother and Grossmamma were "as alike as two peas in a pod," as the old saying goes. It seems her only inheritance from the Fairchilds was her name...Elizabeth. In all other ways she was Grossmamma's child.

Both women had phenomenal physical strength and endurance. Both had "never-say-die" philosophies, and both were very creative in problem solving.

When Father lost everything in the "Crash of '29" it was Mother who pulled us through. "We might be poor for the time being," she said, "but we don't have to *think* poor!" When she emphasized this with a slammed fist on the kitchen table, we all practiced thinking rich.

Now penniless and homeless, we lived by a barter system, exchanging labor for rent and whatever else we needed. This meant much moving, but the family remained intact, each one contributing to the common good.

One day Mother found a formula for making a snowy white, soft soap based cleaning compound which was far superior to the carbolic acid based compounds of the time. She borrowed ten dollars and went into business. The cleaner was a success. She was soon working day and night keeping up with the demand. We had money again. It was the beginning of better times.

As the years went by, Mother continued to meet every challenge with a creative solution and taught her children to do likewise.

She lived to be eighty-nine and her last day found her baking bread for her neighbors.

Grossmamma! Mother! You left big shoes to fill but we are trying.

—M.L.A.

My Goodly Heritage

"The lines are fallen unto me in pleasant places; yea, I have a goodly heritage." (PSALM 16:6)

I HAVE ALWAYS BEEN GRATEFUL that I was born into a family with good "faith genes." I am also glad I was taught early that, "genes" notwithstanding, the most my ancestors could do was to blaze a trail I might follow. But before the journey could even begin, I had to make my connection to God through Jesus Christ for myself. Great great grandfather couldn't do it for me.

The foregoing stories speak of that trail and that journey. The following stories have been shared by fellow pilgrims I have met on the way.

Some have completed their journey and are residing in the city "whose builder and maker is God." Others, are well on the way, while still others are just beginning. All, have a single theme. God!

It is noteworthy that while we can connect with God at any stage of life's journey, those most likely to do it early, are those from solid Christian homes. Homes where they heard the Christian faith expressed in words and lived in deeds.

Today we hear about "family values" as though the whole idea is new. The families that value a right relationship to God, and live that value before their children, are the ones producing the valuable children for the future, as they have in the past.

Read on!

If Your Enemy...

TWO THINGS BECAME CLEAR TO ME the year I was twelve. One was the reality of the Depression that held the country in its iron grip and the other was the nuts-and-bolts of the Christian faith.

Mamma always told us that the reason we did not live like other people was because we were "people of the Book!" I wasn't sure what that meant, but I thought it had something to do with the black, leather-bound Bible that was kept in the bottom of the trunk where important things were kept.

In 1933 we were practically blown out of the Midwest on a cloud of dust. Our part of the country had become known as the "dust bowl." We relocated in the Pacific Northwest, where everything seemed to be the opposite of all we had known. We kept to ourselves and continued to be "people of the Book."

We tried to run a wood lot and Papa learned to file saws. Nothing worked.

We got through the winter somehow and the next spring spaded up a quarter-acre garden plot. We planted the vegetables that fetched the highest market prices. At least, we were on familiar ground. We could take a "stall" at the public market. Others did well. Why couldn't we?

This plan would have worked, but every time a crop matured, somebody came in the night and harvested it. We thought at first it was the "hobos" at a "jungle camp" nearby. We knew it wasn't when the vegetables kept disappearing after the "camp" was vacated. No matter how hard we tried, we couldn't catch the thief.

Finally, Papa went to the pound and got two hungry looking German Shepherd dogs. We kept them in during the day and turned them loose at night. We were all cautioned not to tell anybody we had dogs.

It was time for the cabbage to be harvested, when the dogs paid off.

I was awakened one night by the sound of something bouncing on the back porch and a man's terrified voice screaming, "Call off your dogs! Call off your dogs!" I peeked out the window and saw cabbage heads bouncing all over as they spilled from a gunny sack. I cried as I saw one of our neighbors jump off the porch with the dogs right behind. I buried my face in my pillow when I realized I had helped shell our peas and snap our beans as my best friend, Nick, and I helped his mother when she was canning. How was I to know?

The man was hysterical now and cried again, "Call off your dogs or I'll sue you!"

For answer, Papa raised the window and yelled: "Sic 'em, Dolly! Sic 'em, Queen!"

"You'll pay for this!" the voice sounded farther away now. "I'll see you in court, you rotten, low-down thief!"

Papa didn't call people names, usually, but he had been pushed beyond normal restraint.

The dogs came back with blood on their muzzles and Dolly had a good-sized piece of recognizable pant leg between her teeth. That guy's leg had to be a mess!

"Do you think he will really sue us?" Mamma asked. "Oh, I wish he would! Let him explain to a judge what he was doing on my porch in the middle of the night with a sack of cabbage from my garden...!"

It wasn't so much what Papa said that scared me, it was the way he kept glancing at the rifles on the dining room wall. "There was a time," he growled. "A time...not so long ago...I'd be justified...completely justified...!"

"People of the Book are never justified, you know that. It's not the Master's way." Mamma's voice was firm but calm. It took awhile for Papa to calm down, but he did.

"Has the Master told you what we are to do next?" Papa wasn't being sarcastic. He really wanted to know and he depended on Mamma to tell him.

"He has," she answered. "He said to make sauerkraut."

That was the year we discovered the bounty God had planted in the forest. Restaurants paid a dollar a gallon for blackberries, the produce markets could not get enough mushrooms. Florist shops bought ferns, pine cones, elk horn moss and salal.

"All you need is a little gumption," Mamma told us, "with all this to be had for the picking, nobody should be poor."

Later, when the salmon started returning to their native streams to spawn, we literally camped at a fish hatchery a few miles away. Whoever happened to be there when the eggs and sperm sacs were removed got the fish.

One afternoon, Mamma sent me over to Nick's house with the biggest fish we had brought home that day. "I don't reckon his dad can get to the hatchery with that leg and all."

When I came home and said the leg was badly infected, Papa sent me back with a bundle of slippery elm bark.

"Tell them to take a hammer and pound a little of this to a juicy pulp and put it on the wound," he said. "When it dries out, pound up some more and change it. There is nothing like slippery elm to draw out poison!"

What had happened to Papa? Only a little while ago he said he hoped that thief lost his leg. Him with his night watchman's job at the mill that was so handy, his pension from the war (later called World War I), and the alimony from his wife's first marriage...three incomes... and we had a garden.

"God's garden paid more," Mamma reminded him.

38

That fall I started Sunday School and our very first memory text was Proverbs 25:21: "If thine enemy hungers, give him bread to eat. If he is thirsty, give him water to drink." The rest of the lesson was from Matthew 5:44 "Love your enemies, bless them that curse you, and do good to them that hate you."

Bless Mamma! She was the best Bible I ever read...in any translation.

—J.K.

Our Father

THE FIRST TIME I REMEMBER EXPERIENCING a "move of God" that had no other explanation was when I was eleven. The year was nineteen-thirty-two. Times were worse than bad for our family. There was no money, no work and no hope of getting either.

Our neighbors weren't faring much better, but some of them had faith in a God they called, "Our Father."

Religion had been given the briefest touch in our home. We celebrated Christmas and Easter. We went to weddings and funerals. That was about it. We heard God's name taken in vain in everyday conversation and thought nothing about it. While I was curious about God, He hadn't taken form in my mind. At best He was an idea.

The day that changed all that, I was trying to wake up from a scary dream that seemed all too real.

Loud, anguished cries were coming from Mother's bedroom. I wondered if someone had broken in and was murdering her, but I was too "chicken" to go find out. I covered my head to shut out the noise, but it did no good. The high-pitched voice was yelling at someone. This wasn't Mother's voice! Who was in her room?

What was happening? I started toward the voice and then stopped dead in my tracks. This was Mother and she was yelling at God!

"What do you expect me to do God? Am I supposed to tell my little children their father has abandoned them? Am I supposed to tell them he doesn't care if we live or die? YOU TELL THEM THERE ISN'T A CRUMB IN THE HOUSE TO EAT! IT'S BEEN THREE DAYS NOW...OH! OH!"

She collapsed in a heap on the floor. I left without making a sound and steered my younger brothers and sisters out the door. We could at least play with the dog until things got back to normal.

Frisky was ready for a romp and it felt good to be doing something familiar. I didn't want to believe the words I had just heard, so I put all my energy and concentration into throwing a stick and having Frisky bring it back to me.

"How much would you take for that dog?" An unfamiliar voice startled us. Looking up we saw a stranger leaning over the fence. A lady was with him that we supposed was his wife. They were well-dressed and did not look like the country folk we were used to.

"He ain't fer sale," Buddy answered, scooping the small dog up and holding him tight.

"That's too bad," the man answered as he opened the gate and the two of them came in. "Are you sure about that?"

"He don't b' long to us," Buddy explained. "He b'longs to our big brother, Wilbur. He's out on his paper route now, but he'd be awful mad if we sold Frisky while he was gone."

"Maybe Wilbur wouldn't mind so much if he knew I had to have my dog, MacKensie, put to sleep a little while ago. Mac, we called him. Your Frisky is a 'dead-ringer' for him. It's uncanny, don't you think, Dear?" His wife said it was indeed, but told him not to persist. "They said the dog is not for sale," she said as she took her husband's arm. "We must go now."

Just then, Mother came out to see what was going on. The man introduced himself. "My sister owns Shady Rest," he said, motioning with his head toward the tourist cabins across the road. "We are here off season." Mother nodded.

"I'm trying to talk your children out of their dog, but they said it was no deal. I had to have my dog put to sleep and have been looking for another just like him. As we went for a walk before leaving this morning, I came by and what do you know? There was my dog right in front of me."

Everything happened fast after that. The man left with Frisky under his arm and Mother was holding a five dollar bill.

"Come in, children" Mother said. "I have made some hot pepper tea."

That was a trick Mother learned long ago. Hot pepper tea will stop hunger pangs, sometimes for hours. We drank lots of it in those days. We liked it.

As we were finishing our tea, the couple came back with a box of groceries. "These are a few camp supplies," the man said. We'll get more when we go through town." Then turning to Mother he asked, "Can you get ready to go to town? We'll run you in and back before we go on. You will need to get groceries."

As Mother went to get ready the woman made small talk with us kids. I was grown before I understood why she cried as I explained about the pepper tea. I thought it was information worth passing on.

Mother came back with a lot more groceries than five dollars would buy even in those times. She even had a dollar left over.

The hard part was yet to come. She had to face Wilbur!

Wilbur came home late that afternoon. He had been running errands after he finished his paper route. He brought a bag of doughnuts, some dog bones and fifty cents. His face brightened when he saw the groceries, but fell when he called Frisky for a bone.

Mother explained with tears running down her face. "Oh Honey!" she cried, "I'm so sorry. If there had been any other way...any way at all..." Her voice trailed off and her shoulders shook as she saw the stricken look in Wilbur's eyes.

He was the first to recover. He put an awkward arm around her and said in a husky voice, "Don't cry...it's O.K. ...really it is. We *are* a family, aren't we?"

That scene has played back in my memory many times as people today struggle to define family. What have we lost in these affluent times, that we had in those starvation days? Can we get it back without going through similar times? I hope so!

"You know we couldn't feed him anymore, don't you?" Wilbur asked as I was helping him dismantle Frisky's dog house. I nodded, but we were both near tears. Then, something like an explosion of light happened inside my head.

"Hey, Wilbur!" I yelled. "There really is an 'Our Father.'" Wilbur looked at me questioningly. "Just see what He did," I went on. "He put that guy over in Shady Rest when it wasn't even open. Then He had the guy walk by here so he could see Frisky...the very kind of dog he wanted. Now Frisky has owners who can feed him and we have something besides pepper tea, at least for awhile. Only an 'Our Father' could have mixed every-thing together like that so He could take care of all of us. You do see, don't you?"

Wilbur thought for a moment and then said, "Yeah! He did that all right. Gosh!"

It's the only time I have ever heard the presence of God ac-knowledged in the word, "Gosh," but it was real.

—J.T.

A Different Jungle

MY GREAT GRANDSON, TREVOR, has just left my house and, as always, left me with a lot to think about. He had come to pick up my weekly donation to the food bank his Boy Scout troop is helping to support and to bring the covered dish his mother has prepared for my dinner.

"How is it going?" I asked, as I do every week. "Like it goes," he answered, as he does every week. Then he added something. "It's a jungle out there Grandpa and we all have to do what we can to change things. You never know when one of us could be caught in that mess."

"You are right," I told him. "Nobody ever knows what's around the next bend."

"I put your spaghetti and meatballs in the microwave for you. Just give it a zap when you're ready."

The door slams. He is gone.

As I sat down to eat, I thought again of Trevor's remarks. His choice of the word, "jungle," flushed up a bigger flock of memories from my mind than any flock of quails my best dog ever flushed from the brush.

I am a boy again...Trevor's age. It is 1929. That was the year of the big stock market crash and it seemed the whole country went bust overnight.

My family was lucky. We still had the family farm. Even if prices did go to rock bottom, at least we would eat. Other people weren't so lucky. Men started riding freight trains across the country looking for work. We called them hobos. As they dropped off the trains outside a town, they would set up little temporary stopovers, (called jungle camps), along the railroad tracks, or on the banks of a river, from which they went out over the country looking for work. They would often knock on doors and ask for food in exchange for chopping wood or doing other chores.

The Great Northern railroad track formed one of the boundaries of our farm and just across the tracks was the river. "Jungle Camps" proliferated along both. My older brother, Hal, and I were strictly forbidden to go near these camps, which made them all the more exciting to visit.

That's where I learned to make coffee in a tin can and wrap biscuit dough around a stick and bake it in the coals of a small fire walled in by rocks. I also learned to play the ukulele and sing the "Bum Songs" that were in vogue at the time.

One evening as I was trying to stuff a loaf of bread and a link of bologna into a paper sack, I felt a firm grip on my shoulder and looked up into the stern eyes of my father. If I hadn't noticed the little crinkles around his mouth, I'm sure I would have passed out on the spot.

"Why don't you bring your friends to the house?" he asked. "I'm sure it would beat that 'weed wallow' where they are."

It was the beginning of my parents feeding the homeless of their day. Dad built a long table of planks and sawhorses in the back yard. Mother covered it with bright oilcloth. Hal and I brought the guests. Heaven help anybody who said, "bum" or "hobo" at our house. These were guests. Period.

It never mattered how short our own rations were, we simply added a few more vegetables to the stew or more beans to the baking pot. Mother would put another pan of cornbread in the oven. There was always plenty, no matter how many guests we had.

We made some great friends among these men and many continued to correspond after they went back home. We received snapshots for years from people we no longer remembered.

I feel my eyes burn with tears and wish Trevor could have

44

known the innocence of those times. We were on the tail-end of Prohibition, so there were no drunks in those camps. Nobody had heard of drugs. It was safe for young boys to hang out with "hobos" along the railroad tracks.

"It's a different jungle now," I say to myself.

I think of Trevor and where he goes to help out, not only at the food bank, but in homeless shelters as well and I shudder.

Then I pull myself together before I start to cry and I say: "Of course it's a different jungle, Stupid! It always is. Each generation has its own. It's not the jungle that matters, but how you live in it. You are living right, Trev."

As I wash my dishes I think of my sod-busting ancestors who helped each other conquer their jungle on the Great Plains. It is good to see something so typically American has not been snuffed out yet.

We will survive! We have people like Trevor on the way up!

—V.W.

It Happened at Shiloh

MOST OF THE TIME GOD PROVIDES for us through our own efforts, or through the help of other people. But there are other times (just when we think we have Him all figured out), that He makes a sovereign move that leaves us breathless and, when we think back, we wonder if it really happened.

It seems He must put us aside from time to time and say, "...my thoughts are not your thoughts, or my ways your ways." (Is. 55:8) And again, "...His ways are past finding out." (Ro. 11:33)

I experienced such a "happening" several years ago at my favorite retreat, a Christian dude ranch in Montana called Shiloh. It was a wonderful place and nobody ever came home the same as they were when they went.

Lifetime friendships were forged there. God always seemed so near.

That year at Shiloh there was an unusual move of the Spirit early in the week. It happened, as it so often does, the "climate" was set by one of the campers rather than the leaders, wonderful as they were.

One man shared in the service that as a boy in junior and senior high school he had longed to play first trumpet in the school band. His parents could not afford private lessons for him, so no matter how diligently he practiced, he was "aced out" each year by another boy who took private lessons. He felt worse every time it happened.

"I finally came to hate that kid," he said. "I know that sounds awful, but when you are young, pain can be intense. I was hurting so bad I thought I would die."

"Of course, we grew up and the trumpet was no longer important, but every now and then something would trigger a memory and the pain would return."

"Can you imagine then, how I felt when I met that kid again...right here...in this place...just a couple hours ago? God loved me enough to bring us both here at the same time so I could be healed. Oddly enough, my school rival never knew how jealous I had been or how deeply hurt."

The man dissolved into tears and somewhere in that huge tent another man cried.

From that moment on there was a tender, brooding spirit over the whole camp that opened the way for signs, wonders and miracles.

The days flew by on whirring wings and before we were ready for it, the last day was upon us. We ate breakfast in the dining room and took some fruit with us to have for lunch. The dining room was closing. What about dinner? We would have to eat something before the closing service. We wouldn't have another meal before breakfast on our way home.

I had come with friends, Steve, Trish and their four children and we had shared labor and supplies all week. Now, Trish and I knew we would have to get creative if we had any dinner at all. Maybe the Lord was calling us to fast, but the children would need to eat in any case.

In the portable ice chest we found a package of hamburger that had been frozen and was now thawing, as the ice was gone. There was also a bit of cheese and some odds and ends of vegetables. We decided to go to the nearby store and get a can of taco sauce and a package of tortillas. It wouldn't be a feast, but it would do.

All afternoon campers came by to share and say goodbye. We sang, worshipped and prayed with all who came and went.

By four o'clock the children got hungry so we made up the taco sauce, grated the cheese and opened the tortillas. Our cabin was now full of people playing their various instruments, singing, and praising.

We told the children to help themselves and went back to the "action" in the next room. We were vaguely aware that more children were coming in to eat, but did not pay too much attention.

As people left to go to the final service, some came through the kitchen and seeing there were plenty of "fixings" made themselves a taco.

It wasn't until the last hymn was sung and the last amen was said and we were cleaning up the kitchen in our little cottage that we stopped to wonder where all that food had come from. We hadn't seen anybody bring in any but they must have. How many people had been fed anyway?

A search of the garbage can revealed one eight ounce tin can and the paper from one package of tortillas. We couldn't believe it. We hadn't seen the extra food come flying in, the food that was there just hadn't run out.

When we shared that with the camp director the following year, we learned that such things happened often at Shiloh!

—M.L.A.

Author's note: *I have shared that story many times since it happened so many years ago and have gotten used to the incredulous stares.*

To those brave enough to say: "I don't believe a word of it," I have a stock answer. "That's fine. You need not believe it, but all the unbelief in the world can't make it unhappen!"

I Dared To Be

My STORY OF GOD'S PROVISION is not the story of a single incident, but the story of my life.

I was born in Minnesota in 1912 to a German immigrant farmer and his Norwegian immigrant wife. He was married twice and had a total of twenty-two children. I was number fourteen.

I was born prematurely and failed to thrive for a long time. To make matters worse, it soon became apparent that I couldn't hear. The words, handicapped and disadvantaged are recent inventions used to describe defects of various sorts. In my day we were simply called defective. It was considered a family disgrace to have a defective child. Most families tried to hide the fact as long as possible.

If there had been any help available, pride would have kept a family from seeking it.

It was a foregone conclusion that families would take care of their defective members all their lives. I rebelled against such an idea from the beginning. I had the right to *be*. I didn't know what, but I would *be*!

I didn't know that God had started working on my problem before I was born. My mother was an accomplished vocalist and voice teacher. She got very little money for her lessons, but received many little niceties we could have never bought. Things like cut glass sugar bowls and vinegar cruets, toothpick holders and salt cellars. These added sparkle to her life and she enjoyed them all.

Now, she was fully equipped to give her deaf child a voice. My earliest memories are of sitting on her lap with my small hands on her vocal chords feeling the vibrations as she made sounds with exaggerated lip movements.

She would then put my hands on my own vocal chords and I soon caught on that I was to imitate her lip movements until I felt the same vibrations. She was lavish in her praise when I succeeded. In this way I learned to talk and lip-read. People were often embarrassed when I responded to something they didn't think I'd "heard."

When I reached school age, Mother sent me along with my brothers to the little one room country school. The teacher decided I was "feeble-minded" and treated me accordingly. I got bored just sitting in school with nothing to do. One day I asked for a book and she gave me a dirty, torn book with no cover and told me I could play with that.

I went home in a rage. "Someday she will read a book written by me," I said and I meant it. From then on my mother was my teacher.

She had a few things to say to the teacher. I never knew exactly what was said, but my brothers said I was better off with Mother for a teacher anyway.

It was hard to get used to. She made me work. She knew I

was capable of learning and really sat on me. I got by with nothing. After awhile it was fun. I was proud of my accomplishments. Soon I was reading at a higher level than my brothers and could solve problems in my head before they could get their slates out.

But there was more to my education than the three R's. There was catechism. Being a staunch Lutheran, Mother believed one's soul salvation depended upon being confirmed. You got a free ride until you were twelve, provided you had been baptized. At twelve, you became responsible for your sinful acts and could only make peace with God if you were confirmed.

Catechism consisted of memorizing a ton of scriptures and theological concepts according to Luther. She let me go to the confirmation classes with my brothers, but left nothing to chance. Too little was expected of me by the pastor who taught the classes. I could do more.

I have thanked her all the days of my life for this grounding in faith. I must confess though, I didn't retain much of what I memorized. What I did retain was far better ...an idea. *In God's eyes I was perfect!*

It didn't matter that I was smaller than most boys my age. I had a small mother. I was like her in other ways too. And what was "defective" about hearing with your eyes? God had many ways of doing things and His children did too. I was me. I could dare to be. Be what? Anything God wanted me to be. I just had to find out what that was.

Mother said every human being came into the world with the "seed" for their life's work already planted deep within them. It was up to the individual to find that seed and care for it until it "popped open."

"How do I find it?" I asked. "Look for it among your 'loves'," was her answer. "That thing you love to do more than anything, probably holds the seed."

I had two loves, but I didn't see how a "seed" could be hidden in either one. I love to read and I loved to climb. Of the two, I loved climbing most. My happiest hours were spent swinging from the tops of the tallest trees on our property (which were thirty-five feet or more), yelling like Tarzan. I was also the one who climbed the ladder that was straight up the side of the silo and nailed shingles back on the barn roof after every storm. You might say I was addicted to heights. Where was the "seed" in that? The kind of reading I loved (Zane Grey novels), didn't offer much more.

By the time I was seventeen I was discouraged, almost to the point of despair. My brothers who had left the farm and gone to work on the assembly line at the Ford plant, wrote back to assure me I could never do that kind of work. Nobody wanted me for anything else either.

Then, a steeplejack came to town to paint the water tower and advertised for a helper. I was the only one to apply. I got the job. It was my first and I was proud.

When I saw what that man got paid for that job, after I had done most of the work, the "seed popped open." I left town with him and traveled with him from place to place for nearly two years. He soon discovered I could do more than climb and paint. Thanks to Mother's drilling in mental arithmetic, I was able to estimate the cost of doing a job in my head while Boss was searching for pencil and paper. From then on, I bid for the jobs and did most of them, while he drove the car. He was a drinker, and, in spite of it being Prohibition, managed to find alcohol in one form or another. He was hung over most of the time.

At age nineteen, I cut out on my own. Being in business for myself was great. I never lacked for jobs and made big money for the times. There was one job, however, I always did for free. Any work on a church steeple (from which the term steeplejack originated), was my thank you gift to God for giving me a life. It wasn't much, but it was the best I could do. I was also able to help my parents meet some of their financial obligations.

Only one thing was missing from my overflowing cup of happiness...the affirmation and acceptance of my father. In his own way he was proud and he never turned down any money, but he was also a stubborn man who always had to be right. He had predicted I would never be anything. Having me break his mold he had made for me, was a pill too bitter to swallow.

The steeplejack business has been good to me. It is not an overcrowded field and I doubt it ever will be. It seems God has made only a few who can walk the high places with ease. Maybe some day we won't be needed, but for now, radio towers do need their light bulbs replaced and bridges do need maintenance work. Smoke stacks and flag poles need to be painted. A man who can do these things can name his price and get it.

When I decided I wanted to marry, God had the one and only girl ready and waiting. Alice was an outdoor girl who took to the business like she was born for it.

Now I could bid on two jobs at once. If they both came up at the same time, I took one and Alice the other. Men never seemed to have a problem working under her direction. You might say I liberated her before either of us knew she needed it. We were away ahead of our time.

Our five children, as you might expect, were climbers from the start. For all the years they were growing up, we had a family business. Every summer was spent chasing jobs and doing them together as a family. It was a good life that seemed to agree with everybody.

My greatest joy came when I was able to take my aging mother into my home after Dad died. Only then, did I feel I had paid a little interest on the debt I owed her. She remained with us until she died.

After I was semi-retired, I had time for some of the things I had never been able to do. I served on the Board of Elders of my church and I joined the Gideons. Every desire of my heart had been fulfilled.

Looking back, I don't think I would change a thing. The challenges of my life have made me strong and drawn me into a relationship with God I might not have enjoyed otherwise, so I thank Him for them.

Sometimes I'm invited to talk to school children about my work and I always work in a bit about my life. They don't realize until I tell them that I am, for all practical purposes, deaf. There are noises that get through, but I basically "hear" with my eyes. This always interests them and brings on a lot of questions.

When teachers ask me what advice I would give children about growing up strong, I say the same thing I have always said to my own. "Dare To Be!"

—W.H.

Author's Note: *The foregoing story is taken from the Steeplejack's autobiography, "Fiddle Foot and Free," which I helped him write. He had it privately printed and sold nearly three-thousand copies in five years as he crisscrossed the continent doing his work. "I have realized all my dreams but one," he said one day when a group of his friends were having a pizza party. "What was that?" someone asked.*

"I never found the teacher who gave me an old, dirty, torn-up book when I wanted to read. It would have been the high point of my life to present her with a copy of my book, but she is probably dead by now."

This beloved man has been with the Lord for eight years now. The legacy he left is priceless! I haven't the slightest doubt he is "daring to be," somewhere above the clouds.

The Very Best Christmas Ever

IT WAS ONLY OCTOBER, but we were already planning for Christmas. With a family as large as ours, and a tradition of making gifts for one another, October was none too soon to start.

Our celebrations were always long on heart, but quite short on everything else. It was hard to go to school and hear one's classmates say,. "Is *that* all you got? You '11 have to come over sometime and see what all *we* got!"

To ease the pain a little, we invented a game. When the Sears & Roebuck catalogue came, we would go through it with one another and play, "If I Had A Million Dollars, I Would Buy You..." It was fun and we all grew very generous.

This year, it looked like *that* would be Christmas. The crops had been smaller than usual, the prices lower. Mamma had been able to "do" only two quilts for charity raffles. Even cheap materials were out of reach.

"We can't hold back Christmas," Mamma said, as we gathered around the dining room table for our conference. "It will come right on schedule like it always does, we will just have to do a different kind of planning."

What was she leading up to? We thought we had heard of everything.

"What makes a Christmas gift different than all others?" she probed.

"When it is given to The Christ Child first," we answered.

"Good! You have learned your lessons well. And how do you give to The Christ Child?"

"By giving to those we love and to those in need!"

We had indeed learned our lessons well. There was never a Christmas that we didn't take a sack of potatoes, a loaf of freshly baked bread or a jar of honey to a needy neighbor. It was part of our worship of The Child.

"We have been doing that," she said. "Now it is time to add a new thought, and do something a little extra."

Was she serious? How could we possibly do more than give each other homemade gifts and share from our sometimes meager supplies to help a less fortunate neighbor? Wasn't that enough for The Child?

"You know", Mamma continued, "David said a long time ago in the Bible, 'I will not offer to the Lord, that which costs me nothing.'" II Sam. 24:24

"What does that have to do with us?" I asked.

"Simply this," she answered. "We won't have new materials to work with this year for our gifts, so we will have to do 'makeovers' with what we have. Each of you has a treasure that you can use to make a gift for somebody else."

I was already seeing the "writing on the wall." I had three old dolls, which I didn't play with anymore, but still loved. We *could* put the beautiful head (the one with long curls and go-to-sleep eyes), on the body of another, and add the "Mamma voice-box" of the third and have a doll for Amy.

Part of me was excited over the challenge of making something beautiful out of something old, and another part of me was appalled at the thought of mutilating Pansy, Patsy and Priscilla. It wasn't like I played with dolls anymore. After all, I *was* ten! But these "girls" had been my best friends for a long time.

I went to bed hating David-in-the-Bible and then got scared because hating was a sin.

Dean's "costly" gift was a sack of marbles he fixed for Joey. He had won (over time), a shoe box full of marbles from playing "keeps" with his friends. This practice was frowned upon by parents, but boys did it anyway. This meant, almost every marble had a history of a game where it had been won. There was more at stake than just marbles, but Dean sorted out some of the prettiest "glassies," the very best "steelies," and "dough-babes" that hadn't been nicked. These went into a Bull Durham sack with "Joey" stenciled on the side.

Joey's treasure was a coping saw with a new blade. He was planning to make a bird house in the spring and wasn't going to "use up" the blade on "something dumb."

It was a struggle, but he did "use up" the blade on little wooden animals for Ginny. Then he felt so good, he went into his collection of spools and wooden beads and strung a dozen of them on a long piece of binding twine to make a crib toy for baby Robin. Costly giving was catching on.

Even little Amy had a treasure. An old wallpaper book. She guarded it with her life and screamed "bloody murder" if Ginny looked at it.

Could she give up just two or three pages to make Ginny a book of her own? It took several days for her to come to a decision, but in the end, Ginny had a book of bright pictures cut from old seed catalogues and magazines and Amy had never been so happy.

In the midst of all this excitement, the Sears & Roebuck catalogue came and we nearly drove our poor parents wild, playing "The Game." We were finally limited to an hour after supper.

On Christmas morning, we got a truly big surprise. Dad had cut several lengths from "The Rope," for lariats and jump ropes. "The Rope" was almost a sacred thing. That large coil of hard-twist hemp, hung on a special peg in the barn and woe betide the unwise child who touched it. It was needed for so many jobs around the place. Had Dad actually cut it? It was a costly gift!

Mamma's gift was a big, luscious plum pudding. When she brought it to the table in all its flaming glory, we appreciated the careful saving that had made it possible.

Just when we thought the day couldn't get any better, it did. A neighbor brought a large shopping bag of books that were practically new.

"Walter wants your children to have these," she said. "He got new ones for Christmas."

"How is Walter?" Mamma asked sympathetically, as she served our neighbor with a large helping of plum pudding.

"He's doing better. The doctor thinks he might be able to start getting up some in another month."

We were delighted with Walter's books, but felt sorry for him having to spend so much time in bed. What was rheumatic fever anyway?

When we were going to bed, Mamma pointed out that when we gave The Christ Child a gift that cost us something, He gave back more than we could ever imagine.

"Did David-in-the-Bible know that?" we asked. "He did," Mamma answered.

The lesson we learned that year, stayed with us all our lives, and we always spoke of that Christmas as the very best Christmas ever.

—I.N.

Best Christmas Epilogue

FORTY YEARS LATER, I flew across the continent to spend Christmas with Dean...his last. He knew it. We all knew it. His heart was failing.

"Do you know why I wanted you to come?" he asked.

"So I could hassle you and make your life miserable?"

"That too, but what I really want is to do a rerun of our very best Christmas ever. Could we? It would be the next best thing to going home."

"I don't see why not," I answered. "First we will need gifts for The Christ Child."

"That's been taken care of," Dean answered. "Your airline ticket certainly qualifies, and I have just finished putting everybody's names on those trinkets over there." He waved his arm toward several glass cabinets containing art glass and rare pieces of statuary.

"Still a collector, I see!"

"It's been fun," he said as he smiled.

As I was admiring an expensive amberina flower bowl with matching candlesticks that had my name on them, the doorbell rang.

"That will be the oyster stew I ordered," Dean explained. "We can't have Christmas Eve without oyster stew."

"No we can't, I said."

This creamy oyster stew left nothing to be desired. The accompanying breads and cheeses were perfect and so was the salad that followed. For dessert there were poached pears floating in a bowl of icy limeade.

"Not Mamma's plum pudding," Dean said between bites, "but I guess it will do."

"It will more than *do*. This is fantastic. You are a great host." I could tell Dean was pleased.

"You're tired," I said, after the supper things were cleared away.

"Not at all," he insisted. "We play 'The Game', now."

"Don't tell me you have a Sears catalogue in these "digs."

"No, but I have some "glossies" full of all kinds of pricey stuff. We have a million dollars each, you know."

After ten minutes of playing "If I Had A Million Dollars I

Would Buy You..." it wasn't fun anymore. The old magic that had been created by kids who couldn't buy a new shoelace was gone. So were the "kids." They had been replaced by adults who had done well with their lives and no longer had to make believe they had whatever they wanted.

What I wanted to give Dean couldn't be bought for a million dollars. I felt richer than a millionaire for having had him for a brother.

"Why don't I give you a Christmas foot soak and back rub?" I asked. "You need to go to bed."

"Sounds like a winner, Sis. You always had the greatest ideas!"

As I rubbed his back we talked of home and what had made our childhood special. I assured him "the kids" would be delighted and surprised at the lovely gifts he had picked out for each one. That made him smile.

"It's time to say the verse," I said as I tucked him in. We said it together. "I will not give to the Lord my God, that which costs me nothing."

"I have only one thing left to give," he said. "and I'm not sure it will be accepted."

"And that is?" I questioned.

"Me! What's left of me, that is, do you think it will be enough?"

"I do...more than enough!" I said, trying not to let the tears fall as I thought of the sunshine Dean had spread to others during his lifetime.

He drifted off to sleep still holding my hand. That is how we left each other.

The next day his family claimed him and I flew home. About an hour before the plane touched down, I was filled with "unspeakable joy." I had never experienced anything quite like it.

In that moment I knew Dean's final gift had been accepted.

"How was your Christmas?" my children asked when I got home.

"Except for that other Christmas...back there... whenever it was...it was the very best Christmas ever."

—I.N.

JEHOVAH
SHAMMAH

Ever Present God

OF ALL GOD'S ATTRIBUTES, none is more awe-inspiring than His omnipresence. It can be very comforting to realize God is with us all the time. It can also be very disconcerting.

Jacob experienced this when he woke from his dream of seeing a ladder let down from heaven and angels going up and down. He cried out:

"Surely the Lord is in this place and I knew it not... how dreadful is this place. This is none other than the house of God, and this is the gate of heaven!" (Gen. 28:16 & 17)

When we read the whole story, we see why Jacob was so fearful. He had never been in a worse predicament. But God met him there, and Jacob erected an altar and made vows to God.

David's description of the nearness of God is somewhat less fearful.

"Whither shall I go from thy spirit? or whither shall I flee from thy presence? If I ascend up into heaven thou art there: if I make my bed in hell, behold thou art there. If I take the wings of the morning, and dwell in the uttermost parts of the sea; even there shall thy hand lead me, and thy right hand shall hold me." (Psalm 139:7-10)

Jehovah-shammah! A fact of life to the early Hebrews. But with the passing of time and in changing cultures, this knowledge was filtered out of man's consciousness. We no longer believe that the fear of the Lord is the beginning of wisdom. (Prov. 1:7)

The intellectual climate in which we now live, discourages belief in anything we can't see, hear, smell, taste, feel or touch. But, there comes a time for each of us, when something happens that can't be explained away. Then, we seek God!

The following stories have been shared with me from time to time by people who suddenly met God in an unexpected place or situation and the experience was life changing. In big ways and small, He was there for them when they needed Him. Then, they realized He is always there, just waiting to be recognized.

One lady put it this way: "I never realized God holds our very breath in His hands until I got pneumonia and couldn't breathe. Why did it take that?"

Why indeed? We take so much for granted, forgetting Who does the granting.

Read on and enjoy.

I Walked In His Light

IT HAD BEEN A FUN TRIP. Leah, my college roommate, and I had driven to Canada for a week's vacation before we went to our summer jobs. We had dropped my mother off at my brother, Bill's home in Colville, Washington on the way. Now we were on the way to pick her up.

Leah's old car was held together with scotch tape and paper clips, so to speak, but we were young and naive. If we could get from "point A" to "point B." we asked for nothing more.

Now as we traveled on a dark, country road that had very little traffic, the car began to splutter and cough. We prayed it would make it the next two miles to our destination, but after a final shudder, it died.

After a hurried consultation, it was decided that Leah should stay in the car and I should walk back to the last service station we had passed, and call Bill from the pay phone there. Neither of us had any idea how far back that station was.

As I started to walk down that dark road in the moonless night, I started saying the name of Jesus over and over. Soon I was filled with peace and noticed a soft glow on the road immediately ahead of me. I thought of the phosphorescent tumble weeds that grew in some desert places, but knew that wasn't the explanation.

As I kept calling on Jesus, the glow continued to lead me until I got to the station. Bill came and towed the car to his place where he spent the next day fixing it and we traveled on.

That glow, which was the light of His Presence, has led me ever since.

—L.T.

A Storm To Remember

Nobody living in the Pacific Northwest will soon forget the violent weather that closed out 1996 and lasted well into the new year. The weather here is usually mild...rainy, but mild. We are simply not prepared for nature's fury.

On December 29, the unusual began to happen. An ice storm left our beautiful trees shimmering like crystal. Branches that could not bear the unaccustomed weight, snapped like matchsticks with reports that sounded like gun fire.

The ice was followed by gale force winds blowing in from the Pacific Ocean that were clocked at sixty miles an hour, with gusts to eighty. The snow that accompanied the winds soon blanketed the land. Power outages left people in the dark for days.

When the weather moderated, warming came too fast. Melting snow turned streets into rivers and rivers overflowed their banks. As homes filled with flood waters, people had to be rescued by boat, or from rooftops by helicopter.

Saturated hillsides that couldn't hold another drop, began to slide. Large portions of highways were buried under tons of mud. Expensive homes, built on "view-points" headed for the highway below.

Some people said these bizarre events reminded them of the "bowl judgments" described in the book of Revelation. Indeed it did seem that way.

Did all this happen by chance, or was there a design that could be discerned when one focused on "the big picture?" I choose to believe the latter.

It is nothing short of miraculous that though property damage was counted in millions, fewer than a dozen people lost their lives.

Roofs of stores collapsed when they were not open for business. A marina roof collapsed, sending over a hundred pleasure boats to the bottom of Puget Sound. All were unoccupied.

One man reported watching his palatial home in Seattle, slide down a bluff as he watched a television news broadcast in California where he was vacationing!

The huge mudslide that closed Highway 12, leading into our small town, happened on a Sunday morning between peak traffic hours.

Who but God could choreograph such events with such precision?

My own close call was very small compared to being picked off a rooftop by helicopter, but it was just as important to me.

My husband and I decided to go grocery shopping when it looked like we might be shut in for at least a few days. At the end of our lane he asked, "Do you have the list?" I didn't.

I am one of those people who can't function in a supermarket without a list, so we went back for it. When we started out again, there lay a gigantic tree over the road, precisely where we would have been if we had not gone back for the list.

"That had to be God!" I said to my husband. "I simply never forget the list." "I can think of one other time you did," he answered dryly.

Wow! Two times in twenty-five years! That, in itself is a miracle!

As we began to compare notes with other people, many such stories emerged. One woman whose home was destroyed along with everything in it, put it succinctly.

"All I lost was stuff!"

—B.J.

Storm

It was on New Year's Eve that we all saw the most intricate fine-tuning of events.

Every year on New Year's Eve, fireworks' artists turn the Space Needle in Seattle into a gigantic "Roman Candle." The show, which is televised, gets more spectacular every year. It is timed to start precisely on the stroke of midnight and is coordinated with appropriate music. It's a big event!

This year there was some talk of canceling the show when the weather got so violent, but, in the end, it was decided to go on as usual. Setting it up between wind gusts took some doing, but it was ready on time.

The crowd was smaller than usual, but still, quite a few brave souls stood shivering under umbrellas determined to be there to say goodbye to the old and hello to the new year.

Then, just before midnight, the rain stopped and there wasn't a breath of wind. The "grand pause" lasted for the four minute duration of the show. Never had it been so glorious!

—M.L.A.

Panic Attack

I WAS IN THE FIFTH GRADE when a girl in my class gave a report on the Passion Play that was held every ten years in Oberammagau, a small village in the Bavarian Alps. She said it was given to keep a vow made to God for sparing their town from a deadly plague in 1634.

I do not know why the report made such an impression on me, but it did. Our family was unchurched at the time, and nobody at home ever talked about keeping vows to God.

I made a solemn vow at that time to go to Germany some day and see this famous play.

I had another reason for wanting to go to Germany. Because my maternal great grandmother had immigrated from there, I wanted to see the place I had heard so much about.

I knew that whenever I went, it would take a lot of hard work to save the money, but it was "doable."

The years went by and my life was full, but always, in the back of my mind, was the childhood vow I had made to see the famous Passion Play.

The opportunity came in 1980. A group from our church was joining a European tour, that had the Passion Play as its centerpiece. It would last for two weeks and include many other places of interest to Christians. When I saw the itinerary included a whole day in Rudesheim, I knew I had to go. I could keep my vow and visit my great grandmother's home in one trip! How wonderfully God had planned.

Traveling together with fellow Christians was a great experience. Not only were we having fun but we were learning to know one another better. We also looked out for one another in strange places.

The tour was everything we had hoped it would be. We have all lived with happy memories ever since. Each person had a particular interest apart from the Passion Play. Mine was Rudesheim.

Rudesheim was wonderful and I enjoyed every minute of our time there...that is until the last few minutes.

We were told by our tour guide at every stop how important it was to get back to the bus on time.

"We have a schedule that we must keep," she said, "and we do. If you aren't here, the bus will go on without you.."

All the tourists took this very seriously. We went everywhere in groups and allowed plenty of time for returning to the bus. This time, however, I had gotten separated from my group and when I returned to the bus it was gone. Why? I was ahead of schedule, wasn't I? Then I noticed a small sign that said the bus would load at a different location. Fine, but how did I get there? I was hopelessly lost.

Now, a full-blown panic attack hit me. I was six years old again and my big brother who had taken me to my first day of school had disappeared. I was alone, among strangers for the first time in my life.

My heart raced. My breath seemed to cut off before I could draw in another. I choked and thought I was going to faint. I tried pulling myself together, by telling myself I wasn't six years old anymore. I could cope!

It didn't help. "Oh God!" I cried. "Send someone to find me. NOW!"

The words were hardly out of my mouth when I heard a familiar whistle and my name being called. A man from our group was standing on a little hill above me and was beckoning and smiling. The bus wasn't far away.

In an instant the panic attack was gone. A small thing? To some it would seem so, but I wasn't "some." I was ME!"

The interesting thing is that childhood memory was gone for good. Nothing ever triggered it again. For me there was an added blessing. My mental healing had happened in the place of my "roots." Rudesheim! I think my great grandmother would have been proud!

—M.L.A.

Fly

MY HUSBAND, DON, AND I WERE PLANNING A TRIP to Pennsylvania to visit our son a few years ago. We live on the West Coast and didn't relish the thought of driving across the continent in the winter time. Of course, flying was the only logical way to go, but it was a time of airline disasters and near-disasters. It seemed every time we turned on the news another plane had crashed or had to return to the airport for some reason. We were really getting "bugged."

As the time neared, I asked the Lord for a clear answer to our dilemma, and when the answer came I wanted it confirmed in some way. I didn't want to discover I had "misread" the Lord when we were in the middle of a crisis.

I dreamed that night that we were flying and enjoying ourselves. Was this the answer?

A few nights later we had one of our famous storms. The wind blew with gale force, driving "tons" of rain before it. One of the asbestos shingles on our roof was lifted up, and rain seeped in making a peculiar stain clear across the ceiling. How annoying! We have always been so particular about our home. Now this! There wouldn't be time to paint the ceiling before we left.

I was sitting in my prayer chair still seeking the Lord for confirmation on our mode of travel, when I looked up and nearly jumped out of my chair. Viewed from the angle I was sitting, that stain formed giant letters: F L Y!

I called Don and he saw it too. We took pictures for our friends, not telling them what we had seen. To our surprise, they all saw it too. It wasn't our imaginations. It was the confirmation I had asked for.

Our original itinerary called for changing planes in Minneapolis, but we were told the plane we were to take had lost cabin pressure and would be delayed. We decided to change planes in Detroit instead. The flight was pleasant, just as it had been in the dream.

In Detroit we met a man who had just come in from Minneapolis. "I was on that plane that lost cabin pressure," he said. "We changed planes, and when that one took off, an incoming pilot radioed that he could see something dripping from an engine. We went back to the airport and, sure enough, fuel was dripping from one of the engines."

"We finally got off, but let me tell you, that was one bedeviled flight."

Don and I looked at each other and smiled. We had missed the "bedeviled" flight, by following our inner urges.

We are now serving a two point charge as local pastors in the eastern part of the state and our son lives in our house. He has never painted the living room ceiling. The letters are fading, but they are still there. When you look up at a certain angle, they still spell F L Y!

We need to remind ourselves from time to time, that God's answer is often in the problem staring us in the face. We just need to view it from His angle.

—L.H.

God's Red Light

IT HAD BEEN A MOST FRUSTRATING MORNING, beginning with over sleeping because the alarm didn't go off. I vaguely remembered turning it off sometime in the night. In my haste to get to my bus on time, I slipped in the shower, ran out of shampoo, discovered the cleaners had not sent back the suit I planned to wear, and finally, I broke a shoelace.

I had waited weeks to get an appointment with the company I wanted to work for and it had finally come through. Today was it!

"Oh Lord," I prayed. "Please don't let me miss the bus. You know I can't arrive all frazzled."

The prayer must have worked. I had arrived at the bus stop just as it drew up to the curb. At this time of morning, it stopped only briefly. A few seconds could make the difference between getting on and being left. I got on.

I picked up a newspaper the previous passenger had left in the seat, but I couldn't concentrate. I silently praised the Lord all the way to town and left the bus at the stop across from my favorite restaurant.

Then, whatever fiends had been responsible for the frustrations of the morning, got busy again, or so I thought. The traffic light at the intersection was either stuck on red, or for some reason, was a "long" light. I hadn't remembered it being so. Traffic was piling up, horns were blaring, people were shouting angrily out of car windows. When all this got to be too much, traffic started moving against the light.

There was no way I could get across the street, so I went in to a little coffee shop on my side of the street and ordered coffee and a butterhorn. It wasn't the breakfast I had in mind, but it would have to do.

I was on my second cup of coffee when the sound of a siren caused me to look out the window. Smoke was pouring out of the restaurant across the street where I would have been except for the red light. Firemen were dragging in their hoses, policemen were "shooing" the curious onlookers away. An elderly lady was brought out on a stretcher and put in an ambulance at curbside. It drove off with flashing lights and siren wailing.

After all the excitement, it turned out to be a grease fire in the kitchen and the lady who had suffered smoke inhalation was released that same day.

I went to my interview with a composure I had not felt for months. The stress seemed to have evaporated in the knowledge that I was being protected and cared for by a loving God who would literally stop traffic for me.

There are those who would argue with that idea, but it is real to me. I got the job.

It was later, that I realized I was no longer "stressed out" all the time. Minor frustrations were no longer huge events. A broken shoelace was just that, a broken shoelace, not a "demon" sent to torture me.

Now, when I am tempted to crowd too much into too little time, I whisper: "Red light!" It works every time.

—R.C.

Consider the Lilies
(Matt. 6:28-30)

I HAD BEEN CANNING PEACHES ALL AFTERNOON and was looking forward to getting the last jar in the canner, so I could go for a cooling swim. I was tired and hot and could almost feel the cool water washing over me. How delicious!

At last, the chore was done and I went to get ready for the anticipated swim when a thought intruded itself forcefully into my mind. "Go to the mall, *now!*"

I had just lately been able to "hear the voice of the Lord," and when I acted on the "voice" it proved to be right. With this in mind, I changed into street clothes and headed for the mall.

"I'll drop in on Anne," I said to myself, "she might need an encouraging word."

As I neared Anne's small dress shop, there she was wheeling out a large rack of dresses with a sign: "Summer Clearance." After she parked it by her door, she saw me and called, "I was just thinking about you. Our thoughts must have met out there, somewhere."

"Aren't you rushing the seasons, just a bit? There is plenty of summer left," I said.

"True, but I don't have plenty of space left and the fall merchandise is arriving. Have a look. You might find something you like. Some of them are a downright steal...marked way below cost. Customer wear and tear, if you know what I mean."

I nodded. I knew about "customer wear and tear." A button pulled off...a zipper stuck...soiled spots. It happens all the time.

I found three beautiful, expensive dresses, with just such flaws, now marked one dollar and ninety-eight cents. It *was* a steal!

"Do you ever have a sense of timing!" said Anne, as she wrapped my purchase. "I've always thought it was uncanny, how you always seem to be in the right place at the right time. Now I don't think so...I know so. In a few minutes more the 'madding throng' would have been here and you would never had your pick."

When I left the store, the "madding throng" was all over that rack of dresses. The sign was torn off and hangers were down on the walk.

When I shared the experience with my prayer group that night, one lady said: "Don't you think it is a bit of a stretch to believe our great God would concern Himself with such a trivial matter as your dresses?"

"Why?" I asked. "Does He not concern Himself with the lilies of the field? Jesus said that Solomon in all his glory was not arrayed like one of these. He also said to consider them, and I do...all the time!"

—M.L.A.

A Little Child Shall Lead Them
(Isaiah 11:6)

I CAN'T REMEMBER EVER FEELING SO DESPERATE as I did that morning when I watched my daughter Debra (Debs as we called her) going from door to door in our cul-de-sac, her pony tail flying, her feet dancing.

Debs was five years old today. I had explained to her that I couldn't give her a party and her answer had stunned me.

"I know mommy. Don't worry. I've asked Jesus to send a party and now I've got to go invite the kids." She was out the door before I could stop her.

My husband had left three weeks previous and we were down to the last of everything...milk...bread...oatmeal, and worst of all...hope!

I cried as I watched my little girl making the rounds of her playmate's homes with such joy.

I called the pastor of the church where Debs had gone to Bible school and explained the situation. I asked if I brought my daughter over, if he would tell her that Jesus didn't send birthday parties to little girls.

"I'm sorry," he said. "I can't do that, but give me a few moments and I will call you back."

He called back in ten minutes "A party is on the way," he said, "I called my sister. She will be there shortly."

Just before lunch time, Arlene arrived with a number of paper bags, a half flat of strawberries and a gallon of chocolate milk.

"Here," she said, handing me the strawberries, "clean a bowlful of these. They are better for kids than ice cream."

As Debs watched her every move, Arlene brought out a large box of graham crackers and several bananas. With Debs' help, she made mashed banana, graham cracker sandwiches, which she stacked on a large plate in a tall pyramid. This she topped with five pink birthday candles stuck in fluffy white marshmallows. "Will this be an O.K. cake?"

Debs nodded. "Nobody has ever had one like it," she offered.

"I'll bet they haven't," said Arlene, smiling. "Now run on, Sweetheart and tell your friends Jesus' birthday party is ready."

While she was gone, the table was spread with a paper table cloth decorated in child's party motif, with matching plates, cups and napkins. A honeycomb paper fold-out of a little girl swinging was set in the center.

The graham cracker "cake" and the strawberries and chocolate milk disappeared in twenty minutes.

After the refreshments, Debs opened the gift wrapped packages Arlene had brought. One held three pair of white socks, another, a card of barrettes and the third, a box of crayons and a coloring book.

Arlene then led the children in several choruses they had learned in Bible school, and told them the story of Jesus' outdoor picnic where he fed five thousand people with a boy's lunch. Little eyes were fairly bulging.

As each one left, he or she, was given a bright balloon tied to a children's Bible tract. The last little boy said: "Jesus' parties are funner than ours."

That day marked a turning point in my life. With help from the church, I was able to make a new beginning. But the most lasting lesson I learned, was how to touch the heart of God.

First, you make your request known to God, then you act on your faith. Thanks, Debs. I'll remember.

—O.T.

A Small Miracle

WE USUALLY THINK OF MIRACLES as something big and spectacular like the crossing of The Red Sea, or the feeding of the five thousand with two small fish and five rolls. We sit up and take notice when someone who was dying of cancer suddenly recovers for no apparent reason. These wonderful events are true miracles and we often wish we could experience one.

What we overlook are the small miracles that happen everyday, but we don't recognize them as such. We don't mention them very often because we usually think, "It's no big deal." I know I have done that many times, but there was one I will always remember and though it would seem to be "no big deal," it was a very "big deal" indeed at the time.

I had been in the hospital for a week, spending almost all the time in bed If you've ever done that, you know just how uncomfortable the best bed can become. I could be up a little each day but had to stay tethered to an I.V. Not very relaxing!

Toward the end of my stay, I was allowed up a bit longer each time, which made going back to bed even worse. One evening, as my husband, Russ, was leaving, I felt I had reached the end of my endurance. I looked at my bed and all I could see was a big pile of rocks. My body felt bruised all over. I didn't see how I could lie down in that pile of rocks...not even one more time. Besides the discomfort of the bed, all the noises of the hospital kept me awake.

Tears came to my eyes. I knew I would have another sleepless night. "Oh Lord!" I cried. "Help me to sleep and rest in that bed." Then I reluctantly crawled in. The nursing duties were completed at last and the lights were turned off.

The next thing I knew it was seven o'clock in the morning. I am sure the nurses made their rounds during the night, but for the first time I never heard them. And, wonder of wonders, my body was not hurting!

Yes, it was a "little miracle," but I wouldn't have traded it that night for all the spectacular things I have read and heard about.

I have had many answers to prayer, of course, before and after that time. Usually they come some time after I have prayed and sometimes I don't recognize them when they finally arrive. This incident was so special because the answer came immediately and was definitely recognizable.

"And it shall come to pass that before they call I will answer, and while they are yet speaking, I will hear." Is. 65:24

—D.V.B.

SOMETIMES
HE SENDS
ANGELS

There was a time, not so long ago, when no reasonable person would admit to believing in angels. We were supposed to be beyond superstition. Such fables satisfied primitive peoples who lacked our sophistication and enlightenment. But educated people couldn't accept that which could not be seen or explained in a natural way. That is how the rationale went that I remember.

Now, it is perfectly acceptable to concede that there are things that lie outside the realm of reason as we know it. Angel activity among us has been affirmed once more and the market is flooded with "Angel" books and publications.

I am now at liberty to share stories that have been shared with me over the years…stories of angels coming to the aid of people in times of need. The angel was rarely seen. Its presence was felt or sensed. The result was always the same. The person was never the same again. God was glorified in a new way.

Whose Big, Strong Hands Were They?

I was thirteen when I had finally earned enough money to buy a ten-speed bicycle. Among my friends, a ten-speed was a *must*. Owning one was a "rite-of-passage" from "little kidhood" to COOL! A few blocks from our house was a long, steep hill that ended abruptly on the shoulder of a four lane highway where traffic was always bumper to bumper and moved fast. Needless to say, "the hill" was off limits to young bikers.

I'd had my ten-speed only a few days and wasn't familiar with its operation, when I foolishly yielded to a dare to "do the hill." A few friends came along to make sure I didn't "chicken out" and then just say I'd "done the hill." As I flew down the hill I realized what a crazy thing I'd done. Everything went black in front of my eyes for a minute, and then I saw the highway dead ahead. As my front tire touched the asphalt, I felt strong arms encircle my waist and big hands pressing on my belt buckle. I felt I was being dragged backward and then I lost consciousness.

When I came to, my bike was in a ditch by the side of the road without a scratch on it. I was stunned but otherwise O.K. I picked myself up and walked my bike home, all the time looking for the owner of those big strong hands. I could still feel the pressure on my belt buckle, but whoever had saved me had apparently vanished.

Two weeks after the incident, I got brave enough to tell my mother what happened. She startled me by saying, "Now I know why God called me to prayer so forcefully that day and told me to claim Psalm 91:11 and 12." She got the Bible and showed me.

"He shall give his angels charge over you to keep you in all your ways. They shall bear you up in their hands lest you dash your foot against a stone."

Now I had my answer. I hope to meet that angel some day so I can say, "Thank you." In the meantime, I have the memory of his hands pressing on my belt buckle.

—C.A.

Amy's Angel

WHEN OUR LITTLE GRANDDAUGHTER was four years old, she had a new baby brother. Like most four-year-olds, Amy was lively and noisy. She had to be cautioned about this when her brother was sleeping. Her mother had worked out a system for her when she was out playing and wanted to come into the house. She was to rattle the door handle and someone would let her in. She wasn't to burst in like she had in the past. The system worked well.

One night she had been invited to spend the night with one of her little friends. Her mother was startled awake in the middle of the night by hearing the door handle rattle. She got up and went to the door but nobody was there. Thinking she had dreamed of hearing the rattle, she went back to bed but before she could go to sleep she heard it again. Again, nobody was there. As she started to go back to the bedroom, she heard it again.

Now thoroughly alarmed, she awakened her husband. "We must go to Amy," she said. "Something is wrong. She needs us!"

When they drove into the driveway of the home where she was staying, they could see her inside, looking out the window and crying. She'd had a nightmare that scared her and couldn't wake anybody up. She couldn't reach the phone either, so she went to the window and cried.

The people where she was staying felt terrible that they had slept through the whole thing. But who had rattled the door handle in exactly the same way Amy always did?

To everybody else, it remains an unsolved mystery, but to her parents and grandparents there is an explanation. Amy's Angel saw her need and took care of it. That isn't logical I know, but it is Jesus. Didn't He say children's angels do constantly behold the face of the Father? It's all the proof we need.

—L.H.

The Young Man
In The White Shirt

MY FRIEND, LEONA AND I, had just finished dinner at our favorite restaurant. To our dismay, we discovered when we came out that it had started raining...I don't mean a light rain. It was a downpour!

We ran to the car and got in as fast as we could. We fastened our seat belts and Leona tried to start the car. Nothing happened. She tried again and again...nothing!

As we got out and started to go back into the restaurant so we could call Leona's husband, a personable young man dressed in tan corduroy pants and a white, short sleeved shirt, stepped up and asked if he could help.

"Release the hood," he said to Leona. "I will see if I can find the trouble." He passed his hands over the engine a few times like he was feeling for heat.

"There," he said, "that should get you home, but tomorrow, you should have the alternator checked."

When Leona got the car started, she reached for her purse. "I must give him something," she said, but the young man had vanished.

She asked various people on the parking lot if they had seen which way the young man went and got only blank stares for an answer. "What young man?" they asked.

"We must watch for him on the way home," she said. "He

couldn't have gone far...he hasn't had time."

We looked in vain. We went a couple extra blocks out of our way. There was no young man.

Finally, we decided we had been visited by an angel. Although it was raining "cats and dogs," his hair and clothing were perfectly dry. His voice was pleasant, his manner kindly. He was about six feet tall, had beautiful blonde, wavy hair and handsome features. We didn't know anyone in the area who looked like him. We thought he might be in his late twenties or early thirties. He seemed to know about cars.

The next day when Leona's husband took the car to the garage, he was told he needed a new alternator.

We have talked of this incident often. We still treasure it as one of our most precious experiences. We learned, however, to be very careful who we shared it with. There are still only a few willing to believe, but their numbers are growing every day.

—M.L.A.

Almost A Statistic

A FRIEND OF MINE RECENTLY WROTE: "I am getting sick and tired of all the news reports of rapes, murders, abuse, kidnappings and other horror stories. I have reached a saturation point. Surely something good is happening too."

"Yes," I answered, "something good is happening. God is happening. He never changes. He is here today in the midst of all the evil."

Other correspondence followed, then there came a letter that was different from all the others. The unthinkable almost happened. Evil was no longer somebody else's problem. It had invaded her home.

"Our precious little granddaughter, Jessica, was almost one of those awful statistics you see in the newspapers and on television. I am still shaken." Here is the story.

"I was walking home from my girl friend's house like I've done zillions of times," Jessica began. "It is only six blocks and it was early afternoon. I had no reason to be afraid."

I was nearly home, when a "raunchy-looking guy" in an old beat up pick-up truck pulled alongside me and yelled through the window, "Do you want a ride?" I ignored him and turned around and started walking in the opposite direction, thinking I would go back to my friend's house.

Then this character did a doughnut in the middle of the street, which is highly illegal, and came alongside again. This time, he stopped the truck and started to open the door.

He was laughing real weird-like and said, "No use runnin' kid, I gotcha!"

I was scared! Like paralyzed! I couldn't move and when I opened my mouth to scream, nothing came out.

Then something clicked in my head that I had forgotten. I said, "Jesus!" Just that, "Jesus!"

Right then, the door jammed so the man could not open it. When he started to climb out the window, he looked like he was suddenly in a lot of pain and started rubbing his arm.

That's when I knew Jesus had sent my angel and I hoped he had broken that jerk's stupid arm.

At that moment, I heard a voice saying, "Run down the se-cret trail fast!" I realized I was standing in front of the trail us kids have made so we can cut across lots and get to the next street without going on the road.

I ran like a deer down that trail and I didn't stop until I was in my own house. Then I freaked...majorly.

Two weeks later, a man answering to that same description,

in that same kind of vehicle, tried to pick up two little boys in that same location. They too got away by running down the secret trail.

They ran to school and reported the incident. The principal called the police. This time they got him. When they did, a lot of unsolved crimes against children were solved.

Whenever I share this story, I am met with incredulous stares. Someone is sure to ask: "Do you mean to say that calling the name of Jesus is guaranteed to stop an attacker?" I tell them this life holds very few guarantees, but when one considers the alternative, isn't it worth a try?

—K.H.

"...in heaven their angels do always behold the face of the Father who is in heaven" (Matt. 18:10)

What Does An Angel Look Like?

ANY MENTION OF ANGELS is sure to spark controversy in any group. It seems we want to believe, but are afraid to in this "scientific age."

What do they look like? Do you know anybody who has ever seen one? Could there be a more "logical" explanation for what you saw? On and on it goes. For the skeptic, there are no "logical" answers. For one who has experienced an angelic encounter, there is nothing left to be said. It happened!

In the Bible we read: "Are they (angels) not all ministering spirits, sent forth to minister for them who shall be heirs of salvation?" (He. 1:14)

In Psalm 104:4, David described angels as "ministers of flaming fire."

Three angels appeared to Abraham as young men who came to warn of the destruction of Sodom and Gommorah.

We are warned in Hebrews 13:2 to "be not forgetful to entertain strangers; for thereby some have entertained angels unawares."

It seems from this, that angels, who are spirit beings, can take any form necessary to minister to those who are to be heirs of salvation.

Today, angels are getting a great deal of attention. No longer are people reluctant to share their angel stories. I wish it could have been so, years ago. A relative of mine could have been spared much anguish for believing his dog became an angel for "a split second." This is his story...

Mamma & The Diamondback

THERE WAS NO DOUBT ABOUT IT, Mamma was deathly afraid of rattlesnakes. Today, an analyst would say she was "pathologically afraid" of rattlesnakes. But that analyst wouldn't make a cent, digging around in Mamma's psyche to ferret out the reason for such a fear. Mamma knew why she was afraid.

Her family had come west when she was a child in a covered wagon. Along the way, her beloved older sister, Rosemary, had been bitten by a rattlesnake and died. She was buried in a hastily dug grave in a kindly farmer's pasture, and the family pushed on. Several years later, her father retraced their steps and brought Rosemary back to their new home for a proper burial.

All the grief was lived over again. It had been too much for

Mamma!

Papa always said you would draw to yourself the thing you were most afraid of, and he worried about Mamma and her paranoia about rattlesnakes.

One morning it happened. Mamma was coming back from the well with a brimming water bucket in each hand, when there on the path ahead of her lay a monstrous tightly coiled diamondback, head raised and ready to strike.

She stood, rooted to the spot, waiting for the fangs to sink in, when "from out of nowhere" came a rushing, black and tan blur, and my dog, Brutus, landed flat-footed on the snake's head.

My big brother, Jack, was coming home from rabbit hunting at that moment. He called Brutus away and shot the rattler, but Brutus had already broken its neck.

When that thing was straightened out it measured nearly six feet in length. Jack carried the "rattles" in his guitar for years.

Now here is the strange part. From that day on, Mamma was healed of her obsession with rattlesnakes. I do not know how this could be, but we no longer had to go beating the bushes to make sure no rattlesnake was hiding under them.

She began to talk of Rosemary's life, not death. How good it was to have fresh, new images of this aunt we had never seen. She had taught Mamma to knit and make doll dresses. She had helped her with her spelling.

I decided to write about this incident for "The Washington Farmer," a weekly newspaper that circulated in the rural area at that time.

When I proof-read my story I was shocked to see I had reversed the letters in "God," so they spelled "dog."

"God! Dog! Was dog actually God spelled backwards? Were they the same...really? It made me happy and scared at the same time to think such a thought. Would it make God mad at me?

For years I wondered about the theology of it all. Could God have entered into Brutus, causing him to come to the rescue? No! That would be sacrilegious! If not God, then could Brutus have become an angel for a split second?

I finally settled for that and found peace. I stopped torturing myself with questions I shouldn't be thinking.

But now, a long, long time after the fact, when I think "angels" I see Brutus!

—H.B.W.

I BELIEVE A LITTLE CHILD'S GUARDIAN ANGEL was the prime "mover and shaker" in this next story.

Who knows what person connected to this little one might have cried out to the Lord to send angels to help him? I am convinced someone did for the events to transpire as they did.

I know the writer very well. We have shared many Christian retreats and workshops together over the years. He is open to the Lord all the time. I believe God placed him right in the very spot where he would be needed, knowing He (God) could depend on him to get the job done.

A Cry In The Night

I DRESSED QUIETLY, not wishing to disturb other occupants at this dark, quiet hour: 1:30 a. m. The spartan second floor motel room in the small town had no telephone, and I did not want to be alone, with no phone connecting me with the outside world. Being alone can be satisfying at times, but not when I have some fear about my health.

My life had changed a lot in the last two years. My previous employer had downsized, giving us fifty-fiveyear-olds early retirement and the chance to look for different jobs. My wife agreed to us giving up the security of my regular paycheck. I then landed a job with Joel, a dedicated Christian chemist who had started a company making products from discarded crab shells. The location of the production line was in a quiet southwestern Washington coastal town where I now found myself.

After a normal evening meal, I had settled down in my room for an enjoyable night's sleep. Regrettably, however, in the middle of the night, sleep would not come as indigestion-type chest pains incessantly bothered me.

I was fairly certain that these middle-of-the-night chest pains were just heartburn. But those were the same thoughts my good friend had had recently about his chest pains before he promptly died from a heart attack preceded by his "heartburn." "God!" I breathed, "am I having heart problems tonight, far from home?"

Located a half mile down Highway 101 from the motel was an all night mini market. It would supply me with some antacid tablets, and also provide human companionship and a telephone if I needed to summon aid. It would be a short drive in my pick-up truck.

Outside the motel, as I walked toward my parked truck in the silent parking area, a small voice from the dark highway shoulder whimpered, "Mommy, mommy." I walked toward the sound and found a small boy huddled on the side of the highway. "How could such a small child be out here alone at this time of night?" I wondered. I picked him up and held him close to warm him and quiet his shivering. He couldn't speak well enough to answer any of my questions.

I gave him a ride in my truck to the mini market, where a very kind, grandmotherly clerk comforted him and called the police. An officer quickly arrived. Coincidentally, he had a son this boy's age. He picked the boy up in a tender, fatherly way. They shared a cup of hot chocolate, then the policeman gave him a ride in his shiny police car to the safety of the police station.

I got into my truck and drove back to the motel, pondering these unusual middle-of-the-night events. Then I noticed...my "heartburn" was gone!

"For we are God's workmanship, created in Christ Jesus to do good works which God prepared in advance for us to do." (Eph. 2:10)

—B.W.

Author's Note: *My friend found out later that the child had been with his mother as she was hitchhiking. She had been let out of one vehicle when a trucker stopped for her. She had run to get into the truck and the little one had been "accidentally" left standing on the roadside.*

The proper steps were taken to insure the child's safety from there on out.

It will always be a source of wonder for my friend, that he was there, in the right place, at the right time, to rescue one of God's "little lambs."

I never cease to be amazed at how many different ways our omnipotent God has to get our attention. Just when we think we have figured out how He does things, He surprises us...even startles us.

"For your thoughts are not my thoughts, neither are your ways, my ways, saith the Lord. For as the heavens are higher than the earth, so are my ways higher than your ways, and my thoughts, higher than your thoughts.." Is. 55:8 & 9.

The next story is of just such a "higher happening" that resulted in turning a thoughtless youth back to God...

A Guiding Star

"BEECH 6764U CLEARED FOR TAKE-OFF," the radio squawked in the cockpit.

"Okay, let's get going," said Paul, my instructor.

We had flown from Hoquiam, Washington to Everett, a distance of about 120 miles, to drop off a lady I had been dating. She needed to get home quickly.

I wasn't a licensed pilot yet and so couldn't take passengers up by myself. There was a storm forecast for later in the evening. The weather in the Puget Sound area in December is reasonably predictable...bad! Tonight looked to be no exception. With luck though, we knew the Debonair would get us safely home before the storm closed the airport completely.

As I turned the nose south after take-off, Paul pointed forward and said, "Take a heading of 185 degrees and hold it. We should come in over Elma (a neighboring town with an airstrip just in case we needed it)."

As I reached cruising altitude, I looked out at the horizon. Even though the night was windy, there were almost no clouds in the sky and the stars were spectacular.

Paul, and my Army drill sergeants, had taught me how to use landmarks for navigation. At night, the best ones are points of light. When I saw a pinpoint of light straight in front of the propeller, I asked Paul about using it for a reference point.

"No," he said. "We'll be long past it before we ever get home."

"Oh well," I thought. "I'll use it until another comes into view."

The flight was to take just over an hour, but with cross winds we knew it would take longer. As we flew, we talked about the things we had done that year, about Christmas and the promise of the year to come.

As the flight drew on, I noticed that the light had not grown at all, but neither had it moved. It was still there, at 185 degrees.

About fifteen minutes from Hoquiam, we called for weather and landing. The wind was picking up but it was straight down the runway.

By this time, the light had grown and suddenly I recognized it. Every Christmas a family on the south side of town, puts a huge lighted star in their front yard. That was my guiding light on a windy night flight home.

How had I seen it from so far away? How had it remained so constant...right in front of my propeller?

I don't know. Like many things God does, it's a mystery. What I learned from that experience is that God is always there! Unrecognized...even unwanted at times... He is still there! Perhaps He is only a "pinpoint" of light, but He doesn't move.

Jesus Christ has been Lord of my life for a long time now, and like most people, I don't care to remember every detail of my past. But there is one shining memory that never fades.

Once, at Christmas time, long before I even wanted to be a wise man, I was led by a star.

—D.B.

JEHOVAH
ROHI

OF ALL THE METAPHORS FOR GOD, none is so endearing as "The Good Shepherd." No other image has been so celebrated in art and song. No other gives us such a sense of peace and well-being.

I believe this is so because "deep-down" we all realize we are very much like sheep. Vulnerable, timid, stupid at times. In spite of our proud claim to individualism, we are very much "mass-minded." Under the right circumstances, we will follow any bellwether to destruction.

That's why we need a shepherd. We can't provide for even the simplest of needs by ourselves. We need constant care from the beginning of our days to the end. How comforting to know then, we can be "owned" by the best Shepherd of all...Jesus!

He said of Himself, "I am the good shepherd...I lay down my life for the sheep." (John 10:14-15)

I can relate so well to the Good Shepherd image because my early childhood was spent in sheep country. I remember so well, standing with my brothers by the road in front of our property, watching the huge bands of sheep go by on their way to the summer pasture in the mountains of northern Idaho. The little lambs were so cute as they frisked about and the dogs were a constant source of delight. Responding only to hand signals of the herder, they kept the sheep bunched together as they traveled. The herders too, were real friendly and knew us by name. We came to love them.

On a more personal note, one of my older brothers was a

sheep-herder (they don't call them shepherds in America) in his youth.

The time was the nineteen-thirties. The place was eastern Washington.

The ranchers who had tried cattle there, went broke. They switched to sheep.

CLAUDE'S FAVORITE TIME OF YEAR was in the spring when they took the sheep to summer pasture in the mountains of northern Idaho. It was a break from the tiresome chores of the ranch and a chance to be free for awhile. He loved his job of trail-herder and he loved...actually loved those "dumb sheep."

I never tire of listening to his stories of life on the trail. At age eighty-five, his memories are still sharp and clear. "Trail herding was real adventure," he would say with a far-off look in his eyes.

The route to the mountains lay through the dry, hot canyons that now lie at the bottom of the Grand Coulee reservoir. It is hard to imagine such a thing now as you drive by that long, long, beautiful blue lake, but a whole different way of life lies submerged in its depths.

Punishing though the trip was, it was still the only way to the mountains. The open desert did not have the springs of water these canyons did.

My favorite "trail story" happened on Claude's last trip to the mountains. It was 1936. The Grand Coulee dam was complete and soon the canyons would be flooded to make the reservoir. It was the end of life as the trail-herders knew it. Claude changed occupations at that time. Here is the story...

Good Shepherd's Wisdom

WE HAD BEEN TRAILING FIFTEEN-HUNDRED SHEEP from sunup and it was now near sundown. We would have to find a place to camp soon. There would have to be water nearby, as the sheep hadn't had a drink all day. They were now exhausted and so were the herders.

The trail boss said we would head for Barker's Canyon as he knew there was a good spring there...one that had been dug out. But there was a problem. I had been there the year before and knew the water in that spring was poisonous. We had lost sheep then. We would again.

I begged the trail boss to hike the sheep right past that spring. I told him about the water and told him there was a "sweet water" spring a little farther on.

This made him mad. Who was I to tell the boss where to camp? So, it was in Barker's Canyon that we camped.

My partner and I took a couple of dogs and moved the sheep to a little mesa above the spring where we tried to keep them all night.

It wasn't fun to listen to those restless sheep bleating all night and to see them sniff the air for the smell of water. I wished I could explain to them why I couldn't let them drink. Too bad I wasn't on their mental level.

In spite of our best efforts, a few sheep got away and went to the spring. It hurt me because I knew what would happen.

After the heavy dew fell just before sunup which refreshed the poor animals somewhat, we moved out. We hadn't gone far before some of the sheep started jumping around like crazy and frothing at the mouth. Their bodies stiffened up and their heads swelled up around their nose and eyes, and hung down in ridges. It was an agonizing way to die. We lost a hundred head.

Even now, when I remember those sheep I want to cry. It didn't need to happen. Why wouldn't the boss listen to me? I know I was just a kid, but I was a kid who had been over the trail before. He hadn't.

"We finally figured out," Claude continued, "that it was the *beautiful* lupine that grew in such profusion by that spring that had poisoned the water." One kind of lupine is not poisonous, the other kind is. That's the kind that was growing there.

It was our last trail. After the opening of Grand Coulee Dam, nothing was ever the same again. For those who could now irrigate unproductive land, it was a godsend. For sheepmen it was the end of an era.

—C.T.

Editor's Note: *The spiritual implications in that story are so obvious a novice could see them. There is no need for me to editorialize, but I have thought of those dead sheep often when my Good Shepherd kept me moving when I was sure I couldn't go another step, and when He has not let me drink from a spring that looked so promising, only to find out later it was poisonous.*

I think of the sorrow in His eyes whenever His sheep refuse to be led. Like Claude, He says many times with a catch in His voice: "It didn't have to happen."

On December 23, 1996, brother, Claude heard the final call of his Good Shepherd and he fell asleep in His arms like a tired child. In two weeks he would have been eighty-six.

"With long life will I satisfy him and show him my salvation." (Ps. 91:16)

JEHOVAH
ROPHE

If THE LETTERS I RECEIVE and the personal experiences people have shared with me are any indication, then I believe it is safe to say, more people make a "connection" to God through sickness than through any other means.

Perhaps it is our own pain and suffering that drives us to Him. Perhaps the suffering of a child, parent, husband or wife. Life can go along very well for a long time and it is easy to become complacent. Then, a sudden illness or tragic accident reminds us just how fragile life is and how quickly it can end.

When we are stripped of all our defenses and have nowhere to go, we meet Jehovah-rophe...the God that heals!

Here are a few stories from people who met the Healer and were never the same again.

How I Met The Healer

In JANUARY OF 1980 PAIN CAME ON ME like no time in my life before. What a shock! I had never been sick. I was fifty-two years old, married with three grown children and a grandson. I was employed full time as a maintenance painter for the local ITT Rayonier pulp mill. I had an average active life and was always happy. There had been no symptoms to alert me that anything was wrong.

Life had been good to me. My family was wonderful. I enjoyed the activities of my church and had satisfying hobbies. Chief among these, was being a Teacher-Caller for a square dance club. I was busy and had no plans for being "laid on the shelf."

What then, was causing this pain? If I yawned, I felt like someone was tearing my jaws out of my head. My regular doctor sent me to a specialist at Virginia Mason Clinic in Seattle for a work-up.

The diagnosis was rheumatoid arthritis. I didn't know arthritis came on so suddenly. I thought it sort of sneaked up on you over a period of time. Not so!

I was started on a series of gold shots. I was to take a certain unit of the gold shots over a period of time and then go on a maintenance program of a lesser amount of gold for a longer period of time.

To make a long story short, everything went fine until time for the maintenance program to begin. My joints had improved, the arthritis seemed to be in remission. Then, suddenly, I broke out with what looked like ring-worms all over my body. I was taken off the gold shots immediately. I was put on another medicine that was effective for fifteen days, and then quit working. I was back to square one.

Our church, at this time, started a prayer and healing service on Sunday evenings. I was a believer, but didn't go right away.

I went back to the doctor in Seattle and he put me on a new medicine. He said it would take time to work, so I needn't come back for two months. When I was worse at the end of one month, I decided to try the healing service at the church.

There was a lady there I had never met before (we became good friends later), and she came forward when the invitation was given and laid hands on me and prayed for my healing. She said she would set aside a certain time each day to pray for me and was sure I would be healed.

I later learned our pastor's wife had asked her to do this. Although she had a "healing gift" she didn't want to barge in on her first visit.

At the end of two months, I went back to Seattle for a checkup. The doctor looked at my joints and asked what happened. He said this much improvement could not be expected in such a short time from that slow acting medicine. I told him about the service. He said he believed me, as he had seen it happen that way before. There was no other logical explanation.

It is now 1995 and my arthritis is in remission. I have had two knee replacements, but my hands are O.K. and I don't have the acute symptoms that had made life so miserable. I also have a wonderful friendship with the lady I met that night and we have shared many prayers for various things.

Later, I had back surgery and again, I was covered with the prayers of my wonderful church friends.

Just when I thought I knew all the answers, something happened that was totally unexplainable.

My wife, Evelyn, who was healthy except for diabetes, had a knee replacement, which she came through fine. As she waited all dressed and ready for me to take her home, she died instantly of a heart attack.

I was stunned. She was an active career woman who had more going for her than anyone I knew. It *couldn't* happen, but it did!

Now I am experiencing a different kind of healing. I had heard about "inner healing," for a long time but wasn't sure what it was all about.

Now I know. Soul pain is a lot like arthritis. It can be excruciating at times. Then there is a reprieve. Symptoms recede, you go into remission, but you know the healing will only be completed in heaven.

My wonderful family has been the source of much comfort. My church family has too. I am not bitter, although I miss Evelyn very much. I do not feel God has "let me down." Evelyn is much happier today than she ever was with me, wonderful as our life together was.

Today, my philosophy can be summed up in the words of a much wiser man than I:

"For all that has been...thanks. For all that will be... yes!"

—J.M.

Dream Child

As a young girl growing up I had dreamed, as all girls do, of what I would be when I grew up. Of course, these dreams ran their course and were soon replaced by other dreams, but there was one that remained consistent. More than anything else, I wanted to be a homemaker, wife and mother.

My dream of "Mother" always conjured up a "dream child." I saw myself cradling a rosy cheeked, laughing baby, then, holding a toddler by the hand as we walked in the park and, finally, reading and playing educational games with an eager young learner.

I met my "dream husband" in due time, and after waiting four years, my "dream child" was growing within me. The picture was marred by a troubled pregnancy. Morning sickness lasted every morning and, at times, caused dehydration that put me in the hospital. There were other traumas too, but I took heart from the fact it would soon be over and my "dream child" was definitely worth it.

In time, of course, it was over. Our beautiful little Adam was laid in my arms on my twenty-sixth birthday. What a gift! Our joy was short-lived, however. We were told Adam had "breathing problems" and would have to be moved from our little community hospital to a children's hospital in a larger city.

When I visited Adam for the first time, he was on a respirator and his small body fairly bristled with tubes. As I stroked his thin little hand through the sleeve of the respirator, I remembered the plump, rosy, baby of my dreams and thought: "This is it? So much for dreams!"

Adam was in the hospital for two months as first one thing and then another surfaced. I stayed in a "Hospitality House," nearby during the week and went home on weekends.

Only the sustained prayers of our church friends pulled us through that time that is now a blur in my mind.

I realized just how important that prayer covering was, when I came home one weekend to find the neighbor's house had burned and ours hadn't even been scorched, though the two were right close together. Who but God could have so protected us?

When Adam was finally ready to come home, my husband sent a limousine for us. It was a day of great celebration. The "honeymoon" was soon over. Adam was a fussy baby who wanted to be carried all the time. He'd had a feeding tube for so long, he had "built-in" eating problems.

It seemed all during his first year, he was either fighting off or recovering from upper respiratory infections. He had to be kept away from other children and almost everyone else as well.

If I hadn't been blest with the world's best mother, who stayed day and night for several weeks, I would never have survived, I'm sure. Even as I gave thanks for her, I wondered how others, not so blest, made it.

Now, as I am writing this story, I'm looking back over six years. While I remember the facts, I do not *feel* the pain. God is good! Even the worst of times have a beginning and an end.

Adam has a three-year-old brother now. His name is Cole.

They are very normal brothers who argue and fight at times, but still love each other. Adam has a slight hearing problem, but is otherwise healthy.

As I watch my boys develop, I smile to myself and think: "Dream child number one. Dream child number two." I just have to remember they are God's dream, not mine. Yet, there is nothing about either that I would change if I could.

I have learned we can only dream in broad, general outlines. It is God who fills in the details and colors the picture. Our job is to live expectantly, one day...one dream at a time, giving thanks for all He sends.

—B.J.

Joy Unspeakable

I HAD HEARD ABOUT "NEAR-DEATH" EXPERIENCES for years but paid little attention. If I thought of the stories at all, it was, "How wonderful for that man, or that woman or that child." I didn't know anybody personally who'd had such an experience and I never expected to have one myself. I pride myself on being a "down-to-earth" sort of person and am happy to be present in the "now!"

Then, the unspeakable happened. I had suffered a myocardial infarction, followed by angioplasty and, now, heart failure. My down-to-earth life was coming to an end...fast!

I was in a critical care unit when my cardiologist told my family they could come in and say their goodbyes. There was nothing more they could do.

By this time, I had grown so tired the fight to hang on was no longer worth it. I gave up. I had been a Christian all my life and didn't fear whatever was going to happen. I was aware of my husband and five of our six children gathered around my bed, encouraging me to stay with them, but I was too weary to tell them I couldn't fight any longer.

What I didn't know at the time was that urgent calls had gone out to dozens of prayer chains across the country, beginning with the one in my church, and that a substantial number of prayer warriors were already on the job supporting me and my family as I made my fantastic journey into the "Beyond" and back.

When I decided to give up the fight for life, I found myself irresistibly drawn to a very bright light, that got brighter and brighter as I drew nearer to its Source. My whole being was flooded with an indescribable sense of peace and love. I had never felt so wonderful. My body lying on that hospital bed was totally forgotten.

Then forms began to appear. I realized these were people I had known and loved. My parents! How young they looked! My first husband came toward me with arms outstretched in loving welcome. He smiled. I was about to rush into his arms when I felt another tug. This one was coming from another direction. In that moment I knew my work on earth was not finished. I would have to go back.

No sooner had I made that decision than I opened my eyes and there I was in the intensive care unit with my family around me. "I'm going to make it," I said.

The relief and joy registered in the faces of my dear ones, lifted me up in spirit and gave me a sense of floating above my bed. I was needed still! I was glad I came back. My total recovery followed quickly. My doctors, nurses and everybody concerned with my care agreed it was a bona fide miracle.

Nothing has been the same since. Our whole family has different priorities and has embraced healthier lifestyles.

For my husband and me, every day is an exciting adventure. Nothing is commonplace anymore. A walk on the beach, gathering drift wood, weeding the flowers, listening to rain on the roof, or just sitting by the fireplace at the end of a long day, is a foretaste of heaven. We see with clearer vision, hear with sharper ears, and feel the love around us with heightened satisfaction.

Best of all, is the certain knowledge that for those rooted and grounded in Christ, there is no death. The transition is made as simply as going to sleep in this world and waking in the next. From there on, it is joy unspeakable and full of glory!

—B.B.B.

IF I AM EVER TEMPTED TO FORGET THE MIGHTY WORKS of healing our God performs, I have only to visit my friend, Jackie, at her health food store to be reminded. She, and her husband, who is co-owner of the store, have been more to me than mere casual acquaintances, for a very long time.

As prayer partners, we have a closer bonding, than a more touch-and-go friendship would provide. The relationship is deeper in many ways than some family relationships.

Ten years ago, Jackie survived an accident that might have killed her, or at least maimed her for life. Seeing her going about her business as though nothing had ever happened is a real faith-lifter.

Here is the story in her own words...

Lord Triumphant

WHEN DOES LIFE END AND DEATH BEGIN? In the days ahead I would long for death, but for the moment, I was encased in a cocoon of non-existence. As "life" slowly revealed itself, and "thought" crept into reality like a snail, a shadowy picture remained indelibly etched in my mind. Had I "been there," or was it a vision? My great High Priest, Jesus Christ, had been interceding before the Father for me. Except for His faithfulness, I know I would have died.

Days later, as recovery began, a picture of being on a sandy beach with gentle waves washing over me where I lay, came as a vision. I felt refreshed. Then, in times of confusion, I sensed a chalice filled with a wonderful substance was being poured over me. These were the prayers of the saints now joined with Jesus in His intercessions. It was wonderful. I wanted it to go on forever.

But now I was back. Back from where? How had I returned, if indeed I had been gone? It seemed natural to me to see others walking, but it did not occur to me to wonder why I could not. Time ceased to exist as life flowed on around me. Memory returned in bits and pieces. Would they ever come together again so they made sense? I grasped for meaning in each piece and slowly the big picture emerged.

Our family, consisting of my husband, three of our four teenaged children and I, had been longing for a reprieve from the business that owned us. We had a health food store that was more than a full-time job for us all. We were tired.

Our choice of a place to get away was a happy one. A friend (who was really more like family), had invited us to visit them on their ranch in Montana. They had four teenaged children to match the ages of ours. We all enjoyed many of the same activities. This would be a fun vacation.

We awakened the first morning to the delicious aroma of pancakes and the muffled sound of happy voices. After breakfast, the teens lost no time in getting to the barn and readying the horses for a ride.

It had been years since I had been on a horse, but horseback riding had been a favorite sport when I was a teen. It didn't take long to get into bareback riding again. The mare was a big palomino like one we had when I was young. The ride was pure joy. The sunshine and big blue Montana sky were a delightful change from the "rain capital" of the coast where we lived. All too soon it was time to go back and give somebody else a turn.

As I directed the mare up a short, narrow incline from the driveway to the lawn near the house where the others were waiting, she suddenly started throwing her head wildly. I twisted the reins around my left hand again to try to control her, but it was no use. Welts on her head and neck revealed that bees had been the cause of her panic.

In her terror, she started backing down the incline, still throwing her head wildly. Having already slipped toward her rump, I was in no position to hold on. She lost her footing and we both went down, with her on top of me. Darkness engulfed me. The second wrap of the reins on my hand acted like a noose. As she tried to regain her feet, the weight of my limp body pulled her down and again she fell on top of me. When she finally got to her feet, she kicked me in the head.

I remember nothing of the trip to Hamilton or the race to the trauma center in Missoula. As my husband sat beside me in the ambulance, he remembered another time, years before, when he sat beside his first wife's hospital bed, trying to hold on to her, to no avail. This time, he released me to the Lord and relinquished all claim on me. At this point, I stabilized, after having stopped breathing several times.

As I lay in intensive care, my heart rate would escalate to over 180 beats a minute. My husband and our friend, who owned the ranch, started praying and as long as they did, the monitor showed the heart rate slowing down. If they continued until the rate was about 140 beats a minute, the pattern would break for awhile. If they quit too soon, the heart rate would go out of control again. They said it was interesting to see prayers actually being registered on a monitor. "Watch and pray" took on a whole new meaning.

By now, word had reached the hometown and the prayer warriors there (who were many), started a vigil immediately.

After three days in the intensive care unit, I was moved to a neuro-ward room and physical therapy was started immediately. Retraining new pathways to the brain where old ones had been damaged was the objective. Damage to the left frontal lobe made me appear as though I'd had a stroke.

My right side, from the hip down and areas of my chest, hand and arm, were numb. A basal skull fracture to the left side, escalated equilibrium problems.

I do not remember the initial stages of my therapy, but I was told, I'd have to relearn everything I once knew. How to roll over like a baby, get up on all fours, crawl, pull up to a standing position by holding on to things, and finally, to walk with help. A wide belt was put around my middle for my husband to hold on to as he guided my faltering footsteps down the hall.

It was slow and difficult and I wondered why I had come back. There must be a purpose, but what was it?

The occupational therapist gave me cognitive tasks that were every bit as difficult as the physical. Once familiar tasks like meal planning, making a shopping list, etc. had to be relearned.

After ten days, I had accomplished enough to go home on condition therapy would continue. The doctor had explained to my husband that there were seven stages to recovery and I could stop in any one.

We were fortunate enough to find a therapist in our small community willing to accept the challenges I presented. I went to his office daily and worked hard between visits. In one month's time from the accident, I was back to work part-time. In eight weeks I was working full-time, with no visible sign of having been hurt. Of course, healing would continue for a lot longer, but this didn't show on the surface. I was functional again, even to driving. This had been the final challenge.

Eight weeks! An "eye blink" when you are talking about major brain damage. The medical experts are still confounded.

I have a different relationship with God now than I had before the accident. I met Him in so many new ways.

As Jehovah-shammah, ever present God, He was there when I was hurt and walked with me through all the stages of recovery.

As Jehovah-rophe, my healer, He telescoped time and brought me back to normal living. He did it gently. I don't think I could have stood the shock of an instantaneous healing.

As Jehovah-nissi, my Banner, He is and will always be Lord Triumphant!

—J.O.

JEHOVAH
SHALOM

ALL THE FOREGOING STORIES, lift up that many splendored thing called prayer. It is through prayer that we become connected with God. It is in prayer that we meet Jehovah-shalom, the God of all peace.

Most of us learned prayers in childhood, but they only became vital when we faced a need that nothing else could meet. Then, we discovered Him as supplier of all needs, healer of all infirmities, comforter of broken hearts.

There are others of a scientific mind that approach prayer as a scientific experiment, hoping to learn how it works. Here are a few such stories.

A Weather Prayer

IN THE SPARSELY-POPULATED FLATLANDS of eastern Washington State, our aerospace test technicians were hurrying to complete the liquid fuel plumbing connections and the dozens of instrumentation cable connections necessary to test fire a large, liquid-fueled rocket. Our test station was located in this remote place for various safety reasons, and because of the excessive noise this rocket made when it fired its staccato, rapid sequence pulses.

The rocket was mounted on a stationary, horizontal test stand, and its exhaust plume flamed harmlessly across the desert wasteland. The rocket, which produced 1000 pounds of thrust, represented a new design concept which enabled it to be turned on and off exceeding rapidly, with up to 20 pulses per second of full thrust. The application of this rocket was to steer a new type of highly maneuverable and anti-missile missile which a large defense contractor was proposing to the U. S. Department of Defense. My small company would supply this steering rocket as a part of that missile.

It was Saturday morning, and we were preparing to complete our week's testing series with a recorded-for-TV test firing sequence for presentation to the missile builder. He would then incorporate our test results into his larger proposal. It was our final and most important test.

The flat range land we were located on allowed us to see miles in all directions. For example, we could see rain clouds approaching from miles away, hours before the rain reached our test stand.

Then, on this morning, with about an hour's work remaining to complete the test, a curtain of rain, miles wide, approached us from the far western horizon. After watching its rate of approach, it became obvious that it would deluge us before our test was fired. Because we were testing outdoors in this normally dry climate, our wiring was not rain-proof, and would not function when wet.

Since it was the end of the week, we had no more time left to disassemble the test apparatus for later testing due to our rushed proposal schedule.

Worried about the approaching rain shutting down our final test, I wondered what to do. There was one long-shot possibility. I had read of Christians having their "weather prayers" answered. I even found a Christian woman who went to our church who had had a "weather prayer" answered. It had happened in Hawaii when the family vacation was being ruined by steady, unseasonable rain. An opening had appeared in the clouds above their beach cabin the morning after her nighttime prayer. But she was a dedicated Christian church worker who was unselfish and loving. Much better than I! She *deserved* to have her prayers answered. But what about *mine?*

In my readings about "victorious" Christians who received miraculous answers to prayer, there was a common denominator. God's kingdom was glorified in all cases.

What about our testing situation in the desert? I did not have the nerve to trifle with God, praying for success of a military or commercial situation.

I considered the application of the rocket. It would be used on a defensive missile, not an offensive weapon. It would be used to defend The United States, a nominally Christian nation. This seemed to me justification enough to ask for God's intervention. So I did.

I wandered about the perimeter of our test area, kicking the tumbleweeds as I silently asked God to let us complete our test firing in dry weather. I offered the test to Him, to "make or break" as He saw fit. I would accept His decision.

Our technicians continued their preparations. The rain curtain was only a quarter of a mile away, still miles wide, and moving relentlessly toward us. The smell of moisture was in the air. A few large drops spattered on the ground. The technicians all agreed we would be rained out. As the test engineer in charge, I told them to proceed; that we would conclude the test before the rain hit.

The VCR camera was positioned to show the rocket test stand; our preparations now complete. I glanced at the countryside as we retreated into the instrumentation shed. We were now surrounded by rain on THREE sides. It was raining to the south of us, to the north of us, as well as to the west of us!

We completed the test firing. The test data was complete

and the TV recording successful. We went outside to retrieve the
testing equipment. It was raining...REALLY raining!

"Thanks God," for answered "weather prayers."

—B.W.

Greater Works

I HAD PUZZLED LONG OVER JESUS' WORDS: "He that believeth
on me, the works that I do shall he do also, and greater works
than these shall he do, because I go to the Father." (John 14:12)

I thought of Jesus healing the sick with a touch; feeding five
thousand people with a boy's lunch; calming a storm with a rebuke
and a command; raising the dead!

I thought, greater works than these? I don't think so. Still,
the thought wouldn't go away. What had Jesus meant? Surely He
didn't expect to be taken literally! There had to be a "missing link"
somewhere, but where? I studied diligently and learned much but
found no "missing link."

Finally I decided to try some "lab tests." I would try little
things at first...greater could come later. I told no one about these
experiments. I needed to catalogue the results before saying anything.

It was during this period of time that my pastor called late
one night and asked if I could shelter a young woman and her
baby. She was "at the end of her rope" and had tried suicide. I told
him to bring her over.

It was the age-old story. A runaway teenaged girl had been
found by a "sugar daddy" who dumped her when she became preg-
nant. She moved in with another girl and did the housework in
return for rent since she had no money. Just before the baby was
born, the other girl had taken off with "a great guy," leaving her to

face eviction. No rent had been paid.

Now, with a new baby and no place to turn, she had tried the "ultimate trip" but failed.

The next morning, the pastor called and said he had contacted the girl's parents (who lived in another state), and they were sending plane fare. He had booked a flight for late afternoon but couldn't take her to the airport. I told him not to worry.

I called a friend of mine and explained the situation. I asked if she could drive us to the hotel in a town some fifty miles away, where the airport limousine picked up passengers. She said it would be no problem.

When we started out, the sky was overcast and it was very cold. Since I had been up with the baby all night, I decided to try to get some sleep in the back seat.

I was awakened, or nearly so, by the car sliding and slowing down. I looked out the window and saw we were in a total white-out and hail was falling faster than the windshield wipers could take care of it. It was a dangerous situation.

Still not fully awake, I heard my voice say in a very commanding tone: "Hail! I rebuke you in the name of Jesus and command you to stop, NOW!"

In a few minutes the hail slackened and visibility improved. Then I noticed hail was still falling behind us and in front of us, but none fell on the car! The windshield wipers were turned off.

It continued like this all the way to the town where the young mother and her baby would make connections with the Airporter. We made it in plenty of time.

After a cup of coffee, we drove home under sunny skies and a balmy breeze that felt like spring. It was only February, with much more winter to come, but this was a day set apart for us to remember for years to come.

After entering the data in my "lab notebook," I decided I

was on to something. Was the "missing link" nothing more than taking Jesus so literally, we would use His very words without a second thought? It would seem so.

While we are living in different times and under different circumstances than Jesus, the "power source" remains unchanged. We have the same tools available to us as He had available to Him. A rocket scientist can use them. A homemaker can use them. A child can use them. It's all the same to God. If He had His "druthers" we would all use them more often.

I also understood a little better what Jesus might have meant by "greater works." Certainly the number of people doing His works have increased beyond belief. Who knows how many there are? Not only that, but the modern inventions that we take for granted which speed the spread of the gospel, are greater than anything He had at His disposal during His earthly ministry.

He never used a telephone or sent a telegram. He never appeared on television. He never drove a car or flew in a jet. Yet, all the ideas for these, were resident in Him, just waiting to be released after He had gone to the Father and people had advanced enough to receive them.

I feel so blest that I am living now and can have a part in these "greater works."

The best part of our adventure that day, was that the Kingdom of God was advanced by one soul...the young girl who saw God stop the hail over us, and claimed Him for her own.

—M.L.A.

Strange Calls
& Divine Interruptions

As MY LIFE MOVED FROM SIMPLE BEGINNINGS in prayer to a life of high privilege, I began to experience strange calls and divine interruptions. I never sought visions, but they came. At times they were overwhelming. At other times, I felt deep grief that had no basis in anything that was happening in my life at the time. At other times, I was lifted on clouds of great joy, again without a visible reason. I came to recognize these periods as times when the Holy Spirit was pouring intercessions and supplications through my spirit when my mind was unfruitful. I have learned not to block God in whatever He is doing. I just go with the flow and see where it takes me.

The next few stories describe some of these strange calls and divine interruptions.

Life is always exciting when we live expecting God to do something great and to let us in on it.

But For The Grace of God

Deryk, A YOUNG FRIEND OF MINE, was going through some tough times and his life was out of control. He became obsessed with guns and took marksmanship lessons from an expert. He went around with a gun in a shoulder holster under his coat at all times. I told him that made me uncomfortable and to please not bring a gun to my home.

Finally, an array of problems convinced him he needed counseling and I recommended my pastor. The two seemed to hit it off just right from the beginning and Deryk began to calm down. I told them I would spend their session time in prayer for them if they would let me know when it was. They did.

One afternoon as I sat praying for them in my office at the Christian television station where I worked, a very strange thing happened.

It seemed a large television screen was filling the wall behind my desk. On it, I could see the pastor's office with Deryk seated near his desk. He was wearing a big heavy coat which was buttoned to the chin, although the day was very warm. I knew he was wearing his shoulder holster under the coat. He looked uncomfortable.

Suddenly, he jumped from his chair and went behind the pastor's desk, drew his gun and held it to the pastor's head, right behind the left ear. I gasped in horror. Then I felt the Holy Spirit pouring "violent" prayers through me with such force it made me weak. Deryk went back to his chair and tried three different times to get up and was sucked back each time.

Then the television screen disappeared and my whole being was flooded with peace and joy. I looked at my watch and saw it was time for the session to end.

When I thought Deryk would be home, I called him. He was dumbfounded when I described my experience.

"You will never know," he said, "just how close that very thing came to happening. At first I thought it would be a great joke on good old Pastor B...what a laugh... what a kick! Then, I realized he was right on top of the cause of my problem and was about to bring that secret thing to light. In that moment, I hated him enough to kill him, and tried three times to get up and do just that. I could go behind him and shoot him behind the left ear, before he would know what I was about. Each time, I tried to get out of the chair I was sucked back with a greater force than you feel in a jet plane at take-off."

"When I finally realized what I was about to do, I was horrified and cut the session short. So it was you, intervening. I owe you!"

I told him it was the Holy Spirit intervening and he was a most fortunate young man. I also said I was going to call the pastor and he said to go ahead.

When I called Pastor "B" and told him the story he was truly shaken. He said he'd tried several times to get Deryk to hang up his coat and he said he needed it.

"Believe me, nobody will ever sit in my office again wearing a coat all buttoned up. I will insist he take it off."

He called Deryk and asked him if he wanted to continue the sessions and laid down some ground rules when he said he did.

For Deryk this insight caused him to turn around. He is a family man now and a loving and gentle father. There has been no return to his old life.

That year for Christmas, Deryk gift wrapped a silver bullet and gave it to the pastor with a card that read: "But for the grace of God." The pastor's answer? "Isn't God good?"

Indeed He is!

—M.L.A.

Seeing Beyond

I WAS SITTING IN A PRAISE SERVICE at a retreat in Seattle, Washington, when suddenly the room seemed to disappear and I felt I was standing along a highway. I could feel the hardness of the ground beneath my feet and could smell the rain in the air.

Then, two cars were meeting at an intersection head-on.

There was no way to avoid a crash. One was a small Honda and I recognized the family in it. One I knew well.

I drew in my breath and felt that familiar tug I have come to recognize as the Holy Spirit praying through me.

The little Honda was hit a glancing blow and went skipping across four lanes of traffic; like a drop of water on a hot griddle, missing all the cars in its path.

The mother told her family not to worry, that I was praying and they would be all right.

When all the members of the family were safely out of the little Honda, I was back in the service in Seattle. To my great embarrassment, I was the only one not standing.

"Where have you been?" asked a woman beside me. There was more than a hint of sarcasm in her voice. "Do you sleep that soundly in church very often?" I shook my head no.

The rest of the retreat was very special. I left feeling wonderful.

When I got home I couldn't wait to call my friends and share. I wasn't the least surprised to learn everything had happened exactly as I had seen it. The car was only slightly damaged. Nobody was hurt.

Why do these things happen to me? I don't know. I do know God is no respecter of persons. What He will do for one, He will do for all, but we must be open to the moving of the Holy Spirit all the time.

It is what I mean by a "life of high privilege."

—M.L.A.

The Music of The Spheres

For THE LAST SEVERAL YEARS it has been given to me to hear heavenly music that comes from another dimension of time and space. That is not unusual, really. I know several people who have heard this music from time to time. Every now and then I read a story written by someone who experienced this phenomenon.

What is so special to me is that I hear complete songs that pertain to something going on in my life at the time. These have been taped and a friend of mine who has a music ministry presents them in her concerts. They are always well received. Only the Lord knows how much I treasure this gift.

I grew up feeling very deprived because I had no way to express the music that was inside of me. Our family was too poor to give their children music lessons, even though most of them had musical talents. My brothers learned to play the accordion and guitar by ear and had their own little hillbilly band that was invited to play for country dances and Grange meetings. For me, there was nothing.

Then, during the Depression, the W.P.A. offered free piano lessons. I signed up. It meant walking a total of seven miles to the lessons and then another two to the neighbors to practice.

After six weeks (during which I was doing very well), Dad put a stop to the program. "You are wearing out your shoes too fast with all that walking," he said "and you are getting too late a start to ever do anything worthwhile anyway!"

Only God saw me cry.

I went on with my life, of course, and to make up for the music I couldn't produce, spent a fortune on concert tickets of all kinds. My children had the music and dancing lessons that I didn't have and I had the joy of their various recitals. The emptiness inside me was filled more or less, and I was happy.

One day, without any thought or warning, it happened. The heavens were opened and I heard music such as I did not know existed in any world. There were melodies and counter melodies, harmonies that rolled and lifted in the most amazing way. When it faded away I found myself singing a song I'd never heard before... then another... and another! How does one describe such an experience?

After that, new songs came freely. They were simple songs... very singable...easy for a group to pick up.

My joy is now full. If I could go back and do my life over again I would not change very much. There are rewards for every deprivation.

—M.L.A.

Help!

THE FOLLOWING IS THE STORY of a "divine interruption," my friend, the Steeplejack once experienced on a job. It is one of the most remarkable examples of "supernatural hearing" I can imagine. All the people involved swear it is true. I have no reason to doubt it. Here it is in the Steeplejack's own words.

My son, Warren, an employee and I were painting smoke stacks at a small mill some one hundred-fifty miles from where we lived. Let me tell you that was one noisy place!

There was a high, saw-dust type conveyor that squeaked and squawked its way from the top of the boiler room to the top of a tower. Steam escaping from pipes, noise of saws and trucks were almost vibrating me to death. I could only imagine what people's ears were enduring!

Being deaf has its good points in spite of being unhandy.

Harry was already up on one stack, painting his way down, while Warren and I were standing by a road trying to talk. It was impossible.

Suddenly, from that place inside me, about midsection, that I have come to think of as the "residence" of my spirit, I heard a cry for help! "Listen!" I said to Warren, "somebody's in trouble and calling for help."

Warren turned his head, first to one side and then the other. "That's funny!" he said, "I don't hear a thing."

"Well I do!" I insisted. The cry was getting weaker now and I began to feel panic, as though I were the one needing help.

"Come on!" I said to Warren, as I began to run toward the tower. When he caught up with me, he said, "You're right, Dad, now I hear it too." He started up the ladder and I rushed into the boiler room, yelling like a mad man. "Stop the conveyor!" To my great surprise, they did without asking a question.

I started up the ladder after Warren, and when I reached the top, I was in time to see Warren pulling a man out of a large, disc-like rotating wheel. The man's coat was caught and when each rotation brought him near a system of cogs, he had managed to rear back and yell instead of being dragged in. His only hope was that the steeplejack painting the stack that was on the same level with the tower, would hear him, but Harry hadn't heard a thing. He was growing weaker and had given up hope of rescue when Warren appeared "like an angel dropped from the sky." It took awhile for the shock to wear off and for him to realize he had indeed been saved. If he had been drawn into the cogs, he would have lost an arm at least. More than likely, he would have lost his life. Needless to say, he was grateful.

Now how do you suppose a man with a serious hearing deficiency, had heard that cry for help when it was impossible for anyone else to hear?

That question has been asked many times, not only that day, but for days and days afterward. There is no answer. People just shake their heads in disbelief.

To me, the explanation couldn't be more simple. My Lord, whom I know very well, allowed me to hear...yes, actually hear one word. "Help!" It made all the difference. I know that is not "reasonable," or "scientific," or "philosophical." It's just God being God.

Didn't Jesus say He had chosen the foolish things of the world to confound the wise, and had chosen the weak things of this world to confound the mighty? (I Cor. 1:27)

Then he added with a gleam in his eye, "I don't mind a bit being weak and foolish as long as I see the mighty confounded." A knee-slapping laugh follows that bit of whimsy.

Would that we all could wear our foolishness so well.

—M.L.A. & W.H.

JEHOVAH
NISSI

Triumph in Tragedy

*"And Moses built an altar and called
the name of it Jehovah-nissi."* (Ex. 17:15)

Moses BUILT HIS ALTAR after Israel's stunning victory over
their enemy, the Amalekites. We remember the story, I am
sure, how Moses held up the rod of God during the battle and as
long as he did, Israel prevailed. When his arms became tired
and he let the rod down, Amalek prevailed. Then, two friends
stationed themselves on either side of Moses and held up his
arms until evening and Israel prevailed.

We too, sooner or later, will need Jehovah-nissi. It would be
wonderful, we think, if we could "lie down in green pastures" all
the days of our lives and be cared for by Jehovah-rohi, while
Jehovah-jireh met our every need and Jehovah-rophe healed our
every discomfort. But such is not to be. "Amalek" won't leave us
alone! Not only that, but the Good Shepherd knows the dangers of
an overly grazed pasture.

So, like it or not, we must move out when our Shepherd
calls and the trail runs straight through enemy territory. There will
be battles aplenty. In the heat of the battle, we don't always see
Jehovah-nissi, we just have to know He is there, because He
promised never to leave us. All we can do at such times, is what
Moses did. Hold up the Rod of God...His Holy Word!

When the battle is finally won, we build an altar and call the name of it, Jehovah-nissi. These altars mark the path we travel.

David knew this triumph-in-tragedy and wrote:

"Thou hast shown thy people hard things and caused them to drink of the wine of astonishment." (Ps. 60:3)

But that's not the end of the story. The next verse says: "Thou hast given a banner to them that fear thee."

It has been said that only those whose hearts have been broken, are humble enough to be of use in the kingdom of God. I believe there is much truth in that statement. The people who have touched me most deeply, are those who have known tragedy and heartache.

The next group of stories are from "broken" people. They come from all walks of life. They are young. They are middle-aged. They are old. They are well educated. They are without letters or credentials. All have one thing in common. They are people...people God loves and cares about. They all know "Amalek" well. They know Jehovah-nissi better. They have opened the secret places of their hearts in the hope that others might be healed.

Each one is a diamond, struck by the sun.

The Step Game

"STEP! STEP! STEP! I'm a man-eating tiger coming to get you. Step! Step! Step! I'm a lion, king of the jungle, and I'm going to eat you up."

Andy, my eight-year-old stepson, giggles so I will be sure to find his hiding place. I sling him over my shoulder like a bag of meal and carry him off to bed while he playfully kicks and shrieks and pretends he wants down. I tuck him in, listen to the events of his day and say prayers with him. "Goodnight, favorite Dude," I say, "You know you are my favorite Dude don't you?" "Goodnight, favorite Pop. You know you are my favorite Pop don't you?" I turn out the light after bringing a drink of water, a cracker and his favorite stuffed bunny.

Andy is a real prize after five daughters. At last, there is another man in the house. We do all the things together I dreamed a father and son would do.

Andy never outgrew the "Step Game." Sometimes I would hide and he would be the "wild animal." Whichever way it went, it was always fun.

When Andy was twelve, his mother left me and the two of them moved to another part of the state, but Andy and I kept in touch. I liked the way he was growing up. He was an honor student and well liked by his peers. A natural leader, he was always being elected president of some organization. He was active in church and its youth activities. I participated in his life as much as an absent father can. He was thirteen...fourteen... fifteen.

Then one night when he was fifteen, his mother called choking on tears. "Andy! Andy!" she gasped. "There was a drunk driver...didn't even stop...just kept on going."

"How bad is he hurt?" I asked, knowing the answer, even as I asked.

"He's gone! Oh! Andy..." her voice trailed off in a wail. I sat stunned, trying to absorb the information.

"Step! Step! Step!" Five other men help me carry Andy to bed for the last time. I think of the "Step Game," but this is no game. We move in the slow, measured tread of pallbearers. I am not a man-eating tiger or a lion, king of the jungle. I am a broken-hearted father full of rage. Somebody had snuffed out an innocent life full of promise and just drove on as though nothing had happened!

"Step! Step! Step!" It's time now to lay Andy down among the flowers in that special place prepared for him. Even though I know Andy isn't really there, it's hard to let go. I kneel and kiss the casket. "Goodnight, favorite Dude," I whisper, but there is no answering, "Goodnight, favorite Pop."

As I left the brief service an ocean of grief crashed in on me. I had never felt such pain before. My knees grew weak. I thought I would drown in the tears.

Oddly enough, the tears were not for Andy. He was in a better place. They weren't for his mother or me.. We would heal. No! The tears were for the driver who left Andy to bleed to death on the street. How could anybody live with that? What would life be like from now on? From somewhere deep inside me, a prayer formed.

"Father, forgive him...he doesn't have a clue...not a clue."

The sun came from behind a cloud. Anger floated away. All ill feelings were released. My heart was at rest. I had dealt with my enemy in the only way that had value. He no longer had a part in my life.

The only joy I felt when that driver was finally apprehended was that he wouldn't be out there to kill somebody else's child. He was an "older" man with a long string of D.W. I. arrests. He shouldn't have been out there then, but he was. He could never bring Andy back.

Healing takes time, but it happens. It happens if we let it happen and don't hug our grief to our hearts, refusing to let it go. There came a time when I could remember the joy of having a son for a little while.

All my memories of Andy are happy. How he was "promoted to glory" is no longer important. I know he is fulfilling God's ultimate purpose for his life and that is enough.

Sometimes I remember the "Step Game" and I say: "I'm coming to get you Andy. I will find where you are hiding!" Until then, I won't turn out the light.

—B.D.

A Long Way Home

It was a "seventies thing." God was dead. Absolutes were out. The "new morality" was in. Jesus was expelled from school. Timothy Leary was the guru of youth.

This was the world I entered when I started high school. Speaking of culture shock! This was it! Nothing in my life up to this point, had prepared me for this new world. From a loving Christian home where the gospel was lived as well as preached, I was now constantly challenged by teachers who said they were seeking truth, and urged their students to seek truth also.

"It is time to grow up," they told us. "It is time to lay aside old superstitions that restrict your freedom. You and you alone, are responsible for what you believe. Don't tell me you are free to choose your master, if that choice has to be Jesus!"

"Jesus was, of course, a good man, but who told you He has to *rule* you?"

At first, I was offended. I had invited Jesus into my heart when I was six and had enjoyed His presence ever since. But that was a matter of faith...faith that first resided in my parents. I couldn't prove such a miracle had taken place. I also couldn't prove there wasn't a "kernel of truth" in all religions. What research had I done?

In the name of research, our class was taken to a Buddhist temple on a festival day. Every detail of the ceremony was meticulously explained. There were no similar field trips to a Christian church or Jewish synagogue.

In time, all this began to grow on me. I decided to do my own research. It was time to grow up and find the truth, whatever that might be. I said nothing at home about this. This had to be "pure, objective" research untainted with parental input.

I made new friends who were on a similar quest. Together, we drifted into the occult.

My parents did not approve of my new friends and did everything they could to keep me away from them. Nothing worked. I refused to go with them on vacation trips. My friends who were invited to my home, refused to come. I spent more time in their homes than my own and when my parents brought me home against my will, I ran away. This happened so often, they finally put me in God's hands and let me go.

I didn't realize what a slippery slope I had started down until it was too late to climb back up. Seances were accompanied by drugs and sex. I refused the sex but tried the drugs. I gave them up after so many "bad trips" made me think I was losing my mind. I was sure I had been to hell more than once. I no longer doubted it was real.

My friends drifted away and new friends took their places. Nobody could have found me if they wanted to, for I was always in a different home in a different part of the city.

At last, there was no place left for me to stay. Parents had grown weary and no longer allowed "strange children" in their homes. I was too ashamed to call my parents and ask for a second chance. I had no money and no way to get any. No way that was legal or moral, that is.

That was my condition when I was found by a group of older young people (twenty-something) who said I could join their "commune" if I would do the housework and show the merchandise they were selling to prospective customers.

The "commune" was an old ramshackle building in a down-at-the-heel part of the city and the "merchandise" was whatever a night of burglary netted. It was scary, but it was a living. Nobody was big on paying bills. We were soon without heat and water. Nobody cared. If they could lie around stoned out of their minds it was all they wanted.

I spent eight months in this "commune." I was glad when everybody was gone and dreaded when they would come back. For all their lawless living, they thought of me as a little kid and never tried to involve me in their escapades. As long as I kept my mouth shut about where they got their merchandise and kept the place reasonably clean, I was well treated.

One day, there was a knock on the door and a voice yelled, "Open up! Police!"

There was a mad scramble for the doors and windows while officers rushed in with drawn guns, yelling orders and snapping handcuffs on those they caught.

I was taken to the police station, where I finally called my parents. It had been a total of fourteen months since I had seen them. What kind of welcome could I expect? It never occurred to me, there would be no welcome at all.

"Stay right where you are," Dad ordered. "I'm on my way to get you."

I soon learned it was not possible to go home and expect everything to be just like it was when I left. I couldn't pick up where I left off as though nothing had happened. Too much had happened and we were not the same people we had been. My happy, fun-loving parents were now sober and serious most of the time. I was "flighty" and couldn't seem to settle down.

Too late I learned that the precious, growing-up years, that should have been the brightest and best of my life, were gone and no amount of repentance could bring them back. It had been a bitter forfeit.

The "truth" I had been "researching" needed no such study. It was right there in front of me all the time. Jesus said, "I am the way, the truth and the life, no man comes to the Father but by me." (Jn. 14:6)

I had participated in that truth from early childhood. Atheistic teachers who ridiculed that truth, had nothing better to offer. Neither did any of the cults I visited. I went away to school better prepared than I had been.

I found happiness in a career, marriage and motherhood. Life was full and I was too busy to dwell on the "what-might-have-beens." There was joy today and today was all that mattered.

When my children reached teenage, something quite wonderful happened. As I entered into their activities, as much as they let me, a door in the deep recesses of my mind swung open. I was young again! Now, it was me preparing for the orchestra concert, playing point guard on the basketball team, going out on my first date. I was buying a lovely gown for the senior prom.

As I wondered about all this and hoped I wasn't getting senile, I remembered a long-forgotten scripture verse. "I will restore the years the locusts have eaten." (Joel 2:25) That was it! I was whole again. There were no missing parts.

It had taken a long time, over a long, long trail, but I was home!

—J.A.

The God of All Comfort

It was a strange reversal of roles and totally unexpected, but who does expect to become the legal guardian of one's mother? This was the situation in which I found myself when Mother became too ill with cancer and assorted other ills to make decisions and transact business for herself. We had always been close, but as Mother and daughter, not patient and guardian. Still, I took comfort in the fact that I could now give back some of the care and protection she had given me as a child.

She was able to remain in her own home (which was close to mine), and I could give her the help she needed with her personal care and housekeeping. It was a good arrangement, but I knew she was often lonely. She would never complain, but this left empty hours for her to try to fill.

We were all delighted when our youngest brother (Mother's "baby") moved in with her. He had no family, so he could give all his attention to Mother. He was a good cook and housekeeper, did the grocery shopping, etc. He had the sunniest of dispositions and she loved his wise-cracks and practical jokes. He could make her laugh when nobody else could. He was also legally blind (had only shadow vision) so Mother felt needed again. It was good for her ego to feel they were helping each other.

Unfortunately, Brother had also picked up some bad habits along the way and his friends weren't of the best. He was an alcoholic and had done drugs in the past. It was a combination of drugs and alcohol that had nearly cost him his life, and *had* cost him his eyesight. He had repented at that time and invited Jesus to be his Saviour, but old habits are hard to break and old friends don't drop away easily.

One evening, about a year ago now, Mother called and was very upset. She said Brother was having a party and wouldn't break it up when she asked him to. I could hear the loud music and loud voices and assumed they were all drinking. It sounded like a houseful. Mother wanted to go to bed, but was too uneasy to do so with all the "goings-on." Would I please come and take care of the matter for her?

I went to her home and asked Brother's guests to leave. They did, without an argument. This made Brother very angry and he stormed out of the house. He had a friend who lived in a trailer about a mile down the road from Mother's home and said that's where he was going. I cleaned up the remnants of the party, got

Mother settled for the night and went back home thinking all the while Brother was with his friend and would come home when he got over being mad. Little did I know, that wasn't what was happening.

Brother's friend was a paraplegic, confined to a wheel chair. This made him feel especially vulnerable when people barged in on him, uninvited. He and Brother had been drinking buddies in the past, but now he was "on the wagon" and didn't want anything to do with his old friends. To make matters worse, he was entertaining a lady friend and didn't appreciate Brother's intrusion.

He asked him to leave and when he refused (so the friend said), Friend picked up his gun he kept for protection, and shot him. Whether or not he meant to kill him, we'll never know. Most likely he didn't, but in such close quarters it would have been pretty hard not to.

There was a rumor circulating by the time I got home and I called my sister to find out if she knew anything. She said just what was on the scanner, but she would call the sheriff and see what she could find out.

It was about an hour later, when the news reached us that the rumor was true.

I lost it...big time! I kept screaming, "Oh no! No!" I had a bad case of the "if onlys." If only I hadn't broken up Brother's party. But what about Mother? I was her guardian. If something tragic had happened to her, it would have been my fault. If only I hadn't let Brother leave the house. But how could I stop him? He wasn't accountable to me! If only...if only...it went on to the wee hours while I cried myself into total exhaustion.

Sometime in the early morning, I sensed a very comforting presence in my room and a scripture reference was in my mind. II Cor. 1:3-4

"Blessed be God, even the Father of our Lord Jesus Christ,

142

the Father of mercies and *the God of all comfort;* Who comforts us in all our tribulation, that we may be able to comfort them which be in any trouble, by the comfort wherewith we ourselves are comforted of God."

"...the God of all comfort." I grasped those words as a drowning victim grasps a lifeline thrown to him.

My particular ministry at our church is that of music and worship leader. "Neighborhood Church" is interdenominational and charismatic. Praise singing and "worship in the Spirit" are important elements of each service. I never missed a service during that whole traumatic time. Never had I felt such an anointing as I did during those days when "God inhabited the praises of His people." (Ps. 22:3)

I suppose there were a few who wondered how I could be there worshipping with such abandon while my world was falling apart. But, praise God, most understood that I had to be there to gather strength for the trials ahead. And trials there were.

Mother took to her bed and shut everybody out. She rarely opened her eyes and did not eat willingly. It was like she had already left the world she could no longer tolerate. Two months after we laid Brother to rest, we laid Mother beside him.

There was still more to bear. In a small community like ours that doesn't have much excitement, our story made grist for the media mill for quite some time. Two handicapped friends turning on each other! Wow!

There was a hearing, of course, but I felt lifted above it. Nothing mattered. Nothing was important, but Jesus. In time, even bad things come to an end. New stories take the place of "used" ones. And so it was.

I find myself reading the newspapers and listening to radio programs with more compassion now for the many victims added daily to the long list of hurting ones. I can offer comfort to others now, for I have been comforted. I don't believe we can experience true comforting and healing unless we have been badly hurt.

I feel my music has a greater depth now, than before the tragedy that God turned into such triumph. Through loss, there was much gain. Blessed be the God of all comfort.

—D.R.

Author's Note: *The writer of the foregoing story is a very dear friend and sister in Christ. Her music has been such a blessing to me and her intercessions for me a few years ago when I was very ill, strengthened me mightily. But her greatest witness came when we all saw her "walking in the fiery furnace and one walked with her like unto the Son of God."*

Her family's ordeal reminded me of those strings of paper dolls we used to cut out as children, when after folding the paper just so, we cut out the outline of a doll and then unfolded the paper. There they were, standing in a row and all joined together. Something like that happens whenever a crime is committed. Multiple victims joined together from a single act.

Only "the God of all comfort" can go through the line and heal each one. Bless His name, He does just that!

Domestic Violence
Can Happen to Anyone

WHEN THE HITTING FIRST STARTED, I was so shocked that I couldn't believe it was happening. When he came after me with a garden rake, I knew I had to get out, or I wouldn't live to tell about it. If I had known then, what I know now, I could have seen the signs of approaching danger.

We were living in a tropical climate, the envy of our family and friends. We were in a "dream job" teaching in a Christian school in one of the vacation capitals of the world. It wasn't a struggling Christian school like some places we had served in the past. We were receiving regular paychecks and had a good medical plan. We both had Bachelor's Degrees and he had a double Master's.

Eyes turned when we entered a room because we were an attractive couple. My husband believed in making a good impression. We had an impressive car and the house was always presentable. We were such fakes!

My husband was an abuser. I was his current victim. I was wife number four. I was twenty-four years old and had just spent the worst birthday of my life. I was physically ill and my husband had totally ignored me and the fact that it was my birthday.

The abuse began with unreasonable allegations, twisting my words and actions to mean something that would have never entered my mind. His instructions were followed to the letter, then contradicted. "No, that's not what I said." Enough of this can make you doubt your sanity.

Then came jealous accusations when I arrived home fifteen minutes later than expected. I had to continually "prove my love" for him by apologizing and begging forgiveness for hours on end over something for which I was not responsible. Any word of mine, misunderstood, could "give him a migraine, angina, or another long list of symptoms."

Our once happy life, became a nightmare.

He always managed to talk his way into a job, even though he never stayed longer than a few months in any situation. When his debts and rumors from past places finally caught up with him, he would start looking for a new and exciting place to start over.

That was how we happened to be here in this beautiful, Caribbean paradise with a couple of "plum" teaching positions and a wonderful, supportive faculty and administration. It should have been the best of all worlds, and it would have been, had my husband not started showing the dark and ugly side of his character.

When I protested some of his more outrageous behavior, I was told: "If you are the kind of Christian wife, you say you want to be, you will smile, be gracious and say nothing!" I tried my best to be all that he wanted me to be, but it was wasted effort. Nothing was ever quite right. I could never do enough for him.

That's when the hitting began. Not just a slap or a poke, but a blow that would knock me across the room and leave my ears ringing. He was very calculated about this. He made sure that neither my daughter nor anyone else ever saw what was happening. Sometimes he would lock the door and say, "If you call for help, you won't live till it gets here." He was careful not to leave marks where anyone could see. If I did have a slight bruise, skillfully covered with makeup, I had an excuse for that.

Once I even left. I borrowed the school's van and took my daughter and everything of hers and mine that would fit. I found a place to stay through a friend at church.

Within a few hours, he found us. "Now you've done it," he raged. "You have passed the point of no return. You can not come back."

I was wonderfully relieved and laid down and slept for the first time in months, but it wasn't the end yet.

A couple of hours later, he returned to tell me that if I didn't come back, we wouldn't be able to keep our jobs. He told me to come back between seven and eight in the evening, so the neighbors would be at church and not see anything.

I went back. The situation worsened.

He decided that he needed to get off the island. We would spend the entire summer in Florida, although our ability to afford this was questionable. I told him that if things were to be the same between us, I did not want to go to Florida. I had signed a contract for the coming year to teach music only, something I had wanted to do for a long time. I still had the school yearbook to "put to bed."

He led me to believe that if I "behaved myself" it was possible for us to become like husband and wife again. You see, one of his favorite disciplines for me and my daughter was the withdrawal of affection. We rarely appeared together in public now and were never together at home.

I made the unwise decision to follow my husband to Florida, along with my daughter and our permanent, live-in house guest, a sixteen year old girl, unrelated to us.

The next three days were the most harrowing of my existence. He attacked me with a garden rake and ripped open my thigh; then denied it.

He tried to convince my daughter to stay with him while he calmly told me he wanted me out of his life. He needed my daughter as a "cover" for living together with this unrelated sixteen-year-old girl. He also told me he had spent all of our summer salaries from the school and I would have to "paddle my own canoe."

When I would not leave without my daughter, he took us to a bus station in central Florida. He went back to the house we had rented and packed the things he wanted us to have and then dumped us like so much refuse. How we made it across the continent to my family on the West Coast without any resources is a story all by itself. Suffice it to say, we got very well acquainted with the Lord who kept His hand on us all the way.

In my darkest hour, the Holy Spirit gave me a scripture verse that sustained me...it still does. "The eyes of the Lord run to and fro throughout the whole earth, to show himself strong on behalf of them whose heart is perfect toward him." (II Chr. 16:9)

I'm glad it says "whose heart is perfect toward him." If we had to be perfect in all ways, his eyes would never find us.

"Why did you stay?" I have been asked over and over. "Why didn't you tell anyone?"

Part of the answer is that I had been the victim of not only my husband's abuse, but also of spiritual abuse by the church. I had read books by Christian authors which said that a wife was to obey her husband. Period! If he asks her to do something wrong, then he is responsible. When I tried to reconcile these statements with everything else I read in Scripture, it didn't fit. Certainly our church taught that and men took advantage of the teaching.

Now I believe we are each responsible for our own actions. I do not believe God intends for anyone to suffer abuse at the hands of another. Scripture teaches that husband and wife are to respect each other, and submit to one another in love...treating the spouse's body as his or her own. A husband is to protect his wife, not subject her to physical, mental or emotional cruelty.

Another part of the answer to the question "why did you not leave," is that I was threatened with death if I revealed what was going on. I had never experienced anything like this growing up and so was totally unprepared for such a possibility. It never once entered my mind to go to the police. I have no idea what kind of response I would have gotten in a foreign country.

I tell this story for a number of reasons.

It is important that people realize domestic violence can affect anyone. It is not relegated to the ranks of welfare recipients and the unemployed, or to any particular color.

Domestic violence exists within every ethnic group, income level and occupations. Documentation supports the fact abusers are doctors, lawyers, judges, teachers, preachers, well-educated, educational dropouts, businessmen and derelicts. All human beings are subject to this possibility in their lives.

It is important that people recognize that abuse is not always physical. Emotional scars caused by manipulation and mind-games can be as traumatic and long-lasting.

After my experience, I spent time in counseling to receive the emotional healing I needed before I could participate in any relationship.

I now have a dear, loving husband who treats me with respect and affection. He is very supportive of me and always listens when I say we need to talk about something.

Domestic violence is everybody's business. If you are caught up in this sickness, either as a victim or a batterer, get help. The life you save may be your own!

—K.D.

Taken from "Domestic Violence Hits Home," published by Grays Harbor County Social Services, Domestic Violence Advisory Team. Used by permission.

Author's Note: *K. D. is now a caseworker for the Department of Social and Health Services. She has more empathy than most for her clients who are caught up in the vicious cycle she once experienced. She can also point victims to the way out.*

Of all "faceless crimes" none is more evil than spouse or child abuse. The victims are so helpless, and in a society that demanded implicit obedience for so many years, none so undetectable.

Thank God, that is beginning to change, but we still have a long way to go. As more people like K.D. come forward and say, "This happened to me," we will continue to make progress.

"We will rejoice in thy salvation, and in the name of our God, we will set up our banners." (Ps. 20:5)

I'm A Transcender

"I AM NOT A SURVIVOR, I AM A TRANSCENDER." The impeccably groomed, stylishly dressed, silver-haired lady before us, swept the room with a look that took in everybody, and went on, "There is a difference, you know. Survivors merely get through difficult things, but transcenders rise above the same situations and grow from them. That is what I have come to share tonight and I appreciate the invitation."

It was a special meeting of our support group for battered women. The speaker had come highly recommended and we were not disappointed. She had our attention from the moment she stepped onto the platform. Her story follows:

I was ten years old when my father started taking indecent liberties with me. I was frightened and confused. My father had always been an honorable man. I had loved him...now this!

My childhood ended that day and I entered a world of constant fear. I never knew when an attack would come, only that there would be one. Dad was very creative in dreaming up new ways to satisfy his lust. Each "event" was more bizarre than the last. The worst part of it all for me, was having to keep quiet and not let anybody know what was happening. A tall order for a child, but I was threatened with all manner of dire consequences if I told.

My mother did not know at first, but when she found out she did nothing to stop it. I cannot fault her too badly for that, because in the 1920's the world was far different from today. There were no resources for women and children caught in the clutches of brutal men.

Mother did what most women of that day did. She shut her eyes to what was going on. Still she worried that I might let something slip, so she started a story that I had a "heartbreaking character defect." I was a liar! My word could not be depended upon for anything!

This solved her problem rather neatly, but it didn't leave me anywhere. In time, she began to see me as a rival for her husband's affections and then life really got sick. It wasn't that anything ever came out in the open, but the undertow of feeling nearly dragged me under.

My only way of coping was to live as much as possible in my imagination. I buried myself in books and took imaginary trips to faraway places...my favorite was heaven. I got up close and personal with Jesus Christ. To my great delight, I discovered He could talk to me. It was through the Bible. The Holy Spirit directed me to what I needed, long before I ever took a formal Bible course.

In my mid-teens, God intervened and miraculously delivered me from the situation. My pastor had been contacted by a maiden lady missionary who was between assignments and needed live-in help for awhile. I got the job.

It is still almost unbelievable that my parents were willing to let me go.

That lady became my saviour (small "s"). She not only kept me in church and participating in its activities, she also taught me the social graces and little niceties that mark a person of culture, that my home had not been able to provide. She made me new clothes and helped me develop a sense of style that was uniquely my own. When I graduated high school she helped me get a college scholarship.

Although I lived only fifty miles from my family of origin, it might as well have been a thousand. I was no longer a part of their kind of world.

As time went on, I enjoyed a nearly perfect life. There was

only one "fly in the ointment." Sudden flashbacks to times when Dad had attacked me. They came without warning, as the attacks had, and could cause the same kind of fear for a little while. I thought I would go crazy at times.

At one such time, I "heard" the voice of Jesus say: "How much more of your life are you going to give to that poor demon-driven man? Hasn't he already stolen enough? He abdicated his role as father the day he crossed the line and sexually assaulted you! Now, you owe him nothing, so give him nothing. Every time you yield to the anger welling up within you...every time you rehearse a scene, you are giving him power he does not deserve."

That was a new thought. I was now seeing things from Jesus' perspective. I need not feel guilty for not being able to "honor my father." I had no father! There was only a poor, demon-driven man in the place my father should have been. He needed deliverance.

"What should I do?" I asked.

For answer there came a vision of Lazarus in grave clothes, shuffling out of a tomb. "Loose him and let him go!"

I didn't really understand, but I called Dad by his full name and said, "In the name of Jesus Christ, I loose you. Walk free."

There were no flashing lights; no heavenly music; not even a sense of peace. I had been obedient to the heavenly vision. That was all.

It wasn't long before I realized something significant had happened that day. The flashbacks lost their power and soon stopped coming altogether. I had transcended. The old life with all its unhappiness, no longer existed. The frightened little girl was also gone for good. In her place was a woman who could do anything she wanted to do and be anything she wanted to be.

Two years later, I went home for a visit and could not believe my eyes. Dad was a different man. The climate of the home had changed. The youngest children were enjoying a normal life. Mother said the change had come suddenly and for no reason she could see. I said nothing.

Dad lived another ten years after that and never went back to his old ways. Although we never talked about the past, we each knew that within the silence of our souls, forgiveness had been asked and received.

If I have anything worth sharing with others who are caught in this same evil web, it is, don't settle for being a survivor. You are worth more than that. Be a transcender. Loose your perpetrator and let him go. God will take it from there. Trust Him!

The apostle Paul, who suffered more than any of us ever will, said: "In all these things we are more than conquerors through him who loved us." (Ro. 8:27)

I would never recommend that anyone stay in an abusive situation, no matter what it is, but when you are able to leave, don't take the abuse with you. Mental abuse is bondage also. Don't do that to yourself. When Jesus sets us free, we are free indeed. Enjoy!

—Z.C.

Tragedy Averted

STORIES OF GREAT TRIUMPH coming out of great tragedy will always thrill us, but for me, it is an even greater thrill to have a part, however small, in preventing a tragedy in the making.

Such was the experience of our prayer group that had met at our local Christian television studio on October 29, 1994, for our annual "Pray America" day. We set aside the last Saturday of October to focus on the needs of our nation and national leaders. We also bring offerings for the food bank and other charities to bring our event in line with the "chosen fast" described in Isaiah 58:6 & 7.

We hold worship services throughout the day and the public is invited to attend. Between these services, we try to maintain silence as we focus our silent intercessions as the Holy Spirit leads.

On this particular day, during one of the afternoon services, there came one of those sovereign moves of the Spirit, that rarely happens, when everyone comes into one accord without prior announcement or arrangement.

Prayers were intense...fervent...focused on one object! The White House! Deep intercessions were made for President Clinton, and all who would be visiting the White House then. Saturday usually brings a "bumper crop" of tourists!

The burden we felt was heavy! What was going on? Then, there came a moment I can only describe as something akin to suspended animation! All voices were stilled and we felt like "the world was holding its breath!" The burden lifted in a few moments and "it" was over...whatever "it" had been.

We went home, still under the "anointing" of the Holy Spirit. It was wonderful!

That evening, every television newscast carried the story of a gunman who had fired at a tourist, at the White House, he thought looked like President Bill Clinton. He got off several more rounds before he was apprehended.

All the newscasters used words like "miracle" and "incredible" when announcing that although the place was teeming with tourists, not one was hit!

So that was "it!"

Am I really naive enough to believe that five people on the West Coast, tucked away out of sight, actually prevented a king-sized tragedy in Washington D. C.?

Yes! I am! I believe God's fine-tuning is so precise, that He began His "move" on us just before the first shot was fired. I believe we had the feeling that the "world was holding its breath" at the very moment the gunman was apprehended.

Why should it not be so? God's perception of time and space is quite different from ours. In Him, all time is "now," and all space is "here."

All my life I have heard that when the Master has a task to perform, He uses the tool lying nearest His hand. That day we were, collectively, that tool!

—M.L.A.

So I Send You

AMERICA HAS COME FULL CIRCLE since that hardy band of pilgrims first set foot on the soil of the "New World," in search of freedom to worship God according to the dictates of their own conscience.

Braving the dangers of a stormy ocean voyage to get here and every conceivable hardship thereafter, they labored with strong intention to make their dream come true.

Now, their descendants who have built on the foundation they laid, are taking their own cherished liberty to other worlds to share the dream.

Gone are the old sailing vessels of the pilgrims and the saddle horses of the circuit riders, but the spirit that led them is the same spirit that now leads their children through the sky in jet planes and in jeeps bumping over rugged terrain. Only methods have changed. The quest will never change until all can live in peace and security.

When I think of those rugged pioneers and those who came after, who were willing to lay down life itself to further the cause of Christ, I am reminded of the lines of an old hymn:

"Oh young and fearless prophet, Of ancient Galilee, Thy life is still a summons, To serve humanity."

Every age, since Jesus walked among us, has had its "young and fearless prophets." I am happy to number many of them among my dearest friends.

I speak in particular of those young college students during the seventies, who went as tourists behind the "Iron Curtain," carrying precious Bibles to people who couldn't legally own a Bible. They risked arrest, imprisonment and worse to carry out their task. They were dedicated to their Master with the same fervor as all those who went before them. They also heard Him say:

"As the Father has sent me, so send I you."

One such "young and fearless prophet" kept a journal during his exciting adventure. I offer the story from its pages as a fitting climax to this book.

The writer and his friend came to know the Lord on this trip as they had never known Him before. He was there, in all His manifestations, as they trusted Him utterly every step of the way.

As Jehovah-jireh, He supplied every need. As Jehovah-rohi, He led them as a shepherd in a strange land where they really didn't know where they were going. As Jehovah-nissi, He guarded them at the border crossing, and during their stay in Russia, kept them safe at all times. And overarching all, was the incredible peace of Jehovah-shalom.

Everyone who wants to can experience God in His fullness, as these two did. All it takes is daring!

Bible Smuggler

A FEW MONTHS AFTER MY CONVERSION in November of 1968, I read a book, "God's Smuggler," by Brother Andrew. It made a profound impression on me. Until then, it had not come through to me that God was concerned about our daily needs and actually could and would meet them in direct answer to prayer. That, without a doubt, was because I had never experienced great need. Now, I wept with Brother Andrew as he shared the needs of the people behind the Iron Curtain. My prayer was, "Lord, if you can use me in such a ministry, please do." After that, the Believers "over there" were in my prayers every so often.

During this time, my girl friend, Beth, and I discovered that even though we were growing to love each other more deeply all the time, she had been leaning on me instead of the Lord, so we quietly broke off everything that could lead to marriage. We didn't know if we would get back together, but she saw serving Jesus was more important than our being together.

The signs that followed our breaking off were soon to be recognized. A few weeks later, I got a phone call from a friend, Don, that changed the course of my life.

He said, "Have you ever considered carrying Bibles into Russia?" He said a friend, Tom, felt led to go that summer, but a third person on the team had declined at the "eleventh hour." He said he had been awakened at three o'clock in the morning with my name on his lips, so he called.

I didn't have any clear direction from the Lord on what I was supposed to be doing, and with no wedding in sight, I was open. Still, I didn't want to rush into anything without the Lord confirming it. I hung up the phone and went down on my face before the Lord. He gave me a direct word of encouragement; call it prophecy or whatever. It was beautiful! Then I asked for a word from His written Word and for about two hours He fed my seeking heart with promise after promise from the Bible and showed me examples of how He had led and protected His people who would follow His commands.

The final thing I asked of the Lord was harder to my way of thinking. I dug into my pocket and pulled out seventeen cents. "Lord," I said, "this is my life savings. It's all I possess. You said to give and it will be given, good measure; pressed down, shaken together, men will give into your bosom. (Luke 6:38) I claim that promise for my own." Then I walked across town to a couple who loved me and were starting a Seamen's Mission. They may have thought I was a little off when I gave them my seventeen cents, but they received it with joy and thankful hearts.

I then went back to my room and told the Lord I had nothing to give but myself and if this call was really from Him, He would have to provide the means to go. At least I was free. No ties were holding me.

I shared with my youth group at church and they said they would pray with me. The next day one of the fellows gave me three twenty-dollar bills. The day after one of the girls gave me six fifty-dollar bills. In ten days, by different means, there was a pile of checks on my desk totaling eight hundred dollars.

In two weeks I was gone. Passports which take four to six days at the earliest, came in two days. The visa was paid for and sent out for permission to enter Russia. We didn't know, except by faith, that it would be waiting for us in Helsinki, Finland when we drove through five weeks later.

Beth and family took me to the airport on June 4, and very soon parted with tears. Only God knew if I would really carry Bibles into Russia, or get caught doing it, but we had come to a position of faith in believing God for all of it, and had an abiding peace that was never shaken. God's peace became the hallmark of that whole mission and we went forth in joy.

I connected with Tom in the Midwest where we spent time attending various services and witnessing before we went on.

Finally we were down on the ground in Europe. We were no longer natives but outsiders. We didn't speak any of the languages we heard and had no interpreters, but God knew where we were and what we needed all the time.

Getting along, finding places to eat, etc., was challenging, but God provided. We weren't sure when, or if, we would make contact with someone who could expedite our mission, but it was amazing how the correct guidance came at every juncture. It was in Amsterdam (where we had felt led to go), that we finally made a contact in a restaurant. The waitress told us Brother Andrew's secretary worked at the hostel where we were staying, and that was her washing dishes over there.

Eventually, we met and became friends. She could not invite us to meet the Brothers and Sisters of the Fellowship, but would pray that God would burden someone to do that for us.

The following Monday, the manager of the hostel came up to say in a serious, Dutch-accented English, "I hear you wish to help the Brothers and Sisters behind the Iron Curtain, Yes?"

We shared briefly and then he said, "I make phone call, eh?" In just a minute he was back and said, "You have appointment 9:30 tomorrow morning wiss Brother Andrew's people. That is O.K. wiss you?"

We were overjoyed that the great God of the whole universe knew where we were and cared enough to send guides and make all the arrangements for our mission. It was very humbling.

The next morning, Tom and I headed for the secret address in a near-by town that Mr. Heinen had directed us to. Just walking down the street and discovering that it was tucked away from the public eye sent shivers down my spine.

The director welcomed us warmly and listened to our story. When he asked us how many Bibles we wished to carry and we said 2,000, he said, "Ah yes! But Brothers, that is a border that is very dangerous. They have found things there just lately. Do you have faith for 2,000 Bibles. Faith is the blanket that will cover or not cover what you carry. You must have enough. I will get some tea, ya?"

"Right! Sure! He shut the door and Tom and I slid face down on the floor. We prayed as we had never prayed before. "Oh God, give us the number of our faith." At some specific time I sat back up in my chair and Tom had done likewise. We looked at each other and spoke the same number. Done!

When the director came back with the tea, we were ready. "Do you have a number?" he asked.

"Ten!"

"Excellent! Yes, that is the number. If you are led by the Lord, you may come back as Bible couriers and carry many more Bibles."

We left with joy and the small number of our faith. He told us one Bible would often feed 1,000 people. It is copied and passed to that many. We were much encouraged. And so we carried our precious ten Bibles back to the youth hostel and prepared to go to Russia.

The days sped by as we worked at the hostel, shared fellowship, went sight seeing, and took canal trips. We bought a van and equipped it for travel, cooking and sleeping, bought insurance and got ready to leave.

We pulled out of Amsterdam and drove up the Zuider Zee, across Germany, took the International Ferry to Denmark, and on the next day pulled into Copenhagen. After spending the night in the van behind a big tent of a Pentecostal revival that was in progress, we drove along the lovely coast of Denmark, and caught a ferry to Sweden. From there we drove along the west coast to Oslo, Norway, to find the Jesus People for whom we had an address. We attended a Jesus Music Festival with them for four days, then continued our trip across Sweden. In Stockholm we stayed at a Slavic Mission, and the next day, in answer to specific prayer, got the last place on a ferry to Finland, to leave that very night. We were given sturdy clothes to also carry into the Soviet Union, as the Believers had trouble buying things. Christianity gave them a black mark on their identification papers.

After the ferry ride we drove to Helsinki and picked up our visas. This was our last day in a free country.

Russia is just over yonder and we feel it is a huge jail. We are really alert and have the sweet peace that is so important. We have been praying much for the border guards who will be searching us. Beyond that, we are simply trusting God to cover all the details. On July 6, we got up at 6:30 A.M. and packed up to leave at 8:10.

The border crossing came up suddenly...no signs or warnings that we were even close. It included four separate checks. The weather was about 90 degrees with just a slight breeze. The area was lovely with tall trees and birds singing among them. We went easily through the Finnish check, then more slowly through the first Russian stop. The attitudes of the guards were as different as day and night, with smiles changing to scowls and hostility. We pulled into line at the major security check as the fourth car in line. To the left of the driveway was a low, modern looking building that we soon discovered to be the headquarters of all security. It resembled a giant golf tee pushed into the ground in shape. It was impressive. To our right stood a tall tower that overshadowed all the area around. From the top protruded the barrels of all sorts of guns. We could see men behind them at all times. On the ground were soldiers with more guns. They walked continually around the whole area with the guns off the shoulders ready!

The guards really did a job on the car ahead of us. Searchers had found a cache of nylons, lipstick and perfume. The Finnish woman in the car was hauled into the security building, screaming all the way. Tom and I just looked at each other. Slowly, they worked their way back toward us. There were papers (4 copies) to sign, and to declare all books and things. We finished the paperwork and got out to stretch our legs. Tom dropped a Bible down his pant leg in front of the guards. His expression was so horrified, I knew something had gone wrong. He slipped back into the van and dragged it back up his leg and anchored it with his wallet. Brother Andrew had taught us a prayer. "Lord, you made blind eyes to see, now please make the seeing eyes of these guards blind." He surely did. We had the Bibles stuffed in our pants with our shirts hanging out over them.

As the guards came up, they were unfriendly and gruff. They watched our eyes continually for any signs of nervousness. They went inside the engine area, under the dash and seats. They removed the side panels, the engine cover, poked holes in the headliner, went around the van with mirrors on sticks. They only lifted a few things from my backpack, nothing from Tom's. We joked with the one guard that spoke English, and by the end of the search, he was laughing and having a good time. We were not frisked. God at work!

My feelings at the border were mixed. There was peace and great joy at getting through. There was humble gratitude for such grace. Then, there was heart sickness for the darkness in the lives of people who would not admit Christ. As we rolled through the beautiful country I came to have a desire to reach those lives. I was amazed at the poverty I saw. In this supposed technological nation the people lived in the most primitive houses; often tilted, with broken stairs and sagging fences, yet occupied.

Now, having gotten our Bibles across the border, we faced another challenge...how to distribute them. We heard of Bible couriers who got across the border, only to unwittingly deliver the

Bibles into the hands of the secret police. We must be very careful...follow the leading of the Holy Spirit all the way.

It was in Moscow on day three of our trip, that we made the correct contacts. We decided to go to the First Baptist Church of Moscow service at 6:50 P.M. There was a warm welcome at the door. Just inside we were met by KGB secret police and escorted to seats. Four old ladies were forced to move. After another such move, we had rail seats in the balcony. Such a sight I may never see again. Packed in...standing ...old, old people. An American was speaking for installation of a new pastor. Big choir...beautiful singing.

When scripture was read, many were copying it on scraps of paper. We saw only three Bibles in the whole church of some 1500 people. There were no hymnals and only three people under forty or fifty years of age.

We later learned that one out of ten people could very well be a member of the KGB. At the end of the service, the people sang "God Be With You Till We Meet Again," and as they sang they waved a white handkerchief up and down. We could hardly see for tears.

The KGB usher said, "God bless you," as we turned to leave. On our way out of the church building, Tom and I got separated. I went left. He went right. I mingled with the worshippers, and let the crowd carry me down the sidewalk and around the corner, where I leaned against the wall of a tall gray building.

I held a Bible in front of me and prayed that God would direct the right people to me. Immediately, an older woman veered off from the crowd and came toward me with a smile on her face. I opened the Bible and turned it so she could read a portion.

"Biblen!" she whispered. Tears poured down her face as she thanked me and called me an evangelist. "Spasibo, Spasibo, Evangelum. Amerike. Spasibo." In two minutes all my Bibles were gone but I hadn't counted on the uproar. People came from all over. The noise increased until I was able to convince them they could attract the police and lose their Bibles. They scattered.

I sauntered back to the church building and found Tom had made a contact. We followed a man and his daughter toward a crowded thoroughfare. At the edge we were blocked by racing traffic. The father shouted something and stepped off the curb. The daughter spoke English well and said, "KGB coming!"

She grabbed us both by the hand and headed after her father. Somehow we made it across and dashed off into a park on the other side. We just sat on a bench and looked at each other. As it became obvious we were uncomfortable out in public, they invited us to their home.

We took public transport to their neighborhood, as the girl gave us some ground rules. No talking except by them, especially in their neighborhood. Neighbors would instantly suspect something and turn us in.

Once inside their very humble flat, the girl cautioned us to silence, crossed the room to shut the window, pulled the shade and only then turned on the light. They both grabbed us and hugged us several times.

She was Iya, and he was Leonid (not their real names). She went to fix food and apologized for not having jam for the very dry bread and that there was no sugar for the tea. One bag made a very big pot. We called it a feast. She played her guitar that she had gotten from a Western missionary. We sang and they shared some of their story and we shared some of ours. Finally we agreed to meet the next day and go to the country. They took us back to the van and left us.

We picked them up next day and drove into the country many miles. We drove past what had once been a country home they had lived in. It had been taken from them. In a meadow surrounded by trees, we parked the van. We sang and laughed and shared Jesus for several hours. At one point a group that came after we got there, heard what we were singing and saying, with obvious disapproval, leapt up, loaded their car and drove off in a cloud of dust. That sobered us quite a bit.

The blessing of being with this girl and her father was that they showed a courage and commitment we had never seen before.

The Communists had influenced his wife to leave him, taking their young son with her. She was not a strong believer. Iya stayed with her father and, together, they witnessed for the Lord. She would take her guitar to a local park and sing and witness there. She often came home with torn clothes, bruised and bloody from the Cosomal...the young Communists.

Iya sang like a sixty year old woman. What a voice! She was free because she had counted the cost and was willing to die for her Saviour, as was her father.

We met one last time at their flat. The father asked in Russian if we could pray. When we nodded, he flung himself flat on the floor. We followed with Iya lying between us and interpreting. He poured out his heart to God.

"Oh God, make me small so you can use me. Thank you for these wonderful men who have come from America. Thank you that you have not forgotten us. Thank you that you have answered prayer by sending them to us." He prayed for the KGB who guarded his wife and son. As he prayed for America and called us a "lighthouse to the world," I couldn't handle it. My tears mingled with Iya's and Leonid's. Tom and I tried to pray, but God had to read our hearts because it was so hard to speak.

Finally it was time to leave. We gave them the rest of the Bibles, clothes and personal things like soap and shaving gear we had gotten from the Slavic Mission and all the rubles we could spare. You would have thought it was a fortune by the way they acted. The Bibles would be two hundred kilometers away by the next day.

When we returned from Russia, we came back out through Finland again, to Sweden and on down to Holland. We couldn't sell the van, so we drove south to a mission called "Hands to Serve," in Strijen, Holland. These people gave us enough for the van to enable us to fly home.

People tell me that trip to Russia changed me and they are right. How could such experiences not change me? It took living in a police state, just for a little while, to make me understand freedom.

No longer was "oppression" just a word. Oppression had a "face." A face that looked like an old man named Leonid who lost everything...home...wife...son. Also a face that looked like his daughter, Iya, a young woman growing old before her time.

Hunger was no longer something that happened between meals. Hunger was small pieces of hard bread and a tea bag making a huge pot of tea.

No longer was Bible reading a "duty" of Christians. A Bible was precious, worth copying so it could be shared by many, as it was passed through secret channels.

When I got back to America it was hard to sleep on a soft bed or eat more than I needed. The things we take for granted as our "rights" are privileges without price.

I believe we all must change if we are to preserve what we now have. There can be no let-down in principles... no hoarding of resources...no casual handling of our precious freedoms.

"God make us willing to accept the challenge and march on!"

—B.G.

Author's Note: *Yesterday's "Bible Smuggler" is today's owner-manager of a Christian Cable Television Ministry. He and Beth were married after his trip to Russia and, together, they are raising three children. The "faith" lessons he learned early in life, laid the foundation for his present "faith" ministry.*

His great adventure of smuggling Bibles behind the Iron Curtain is now a fading memory. For those who received the Bibles, the memory will never fade.

The Master for whom that great army of student tourists risked their lives, has not forgotten either. One day they will stand before Him and hear Him say: "Come you blessed of my Father, you have been faithful over few things, I will make you ruler over many." (Matt. 25:21)

GOD'S
GREATEST
MOVE YET

IT IS GOOD TO STOP EVERY NOW AND THEN, look back over the way we have come, reflect on God's "moves" in the past and share our experiences with others. But, that was *then*! We are living *now*! What is God doing *today*? Will there ever be another world-changing "move" of God that can compare to those of the past?

In my opinion, the answer is yes! His greatest "move" of all time is happening now, right before our eyes.

What is it, you ask? You are going to love this. The Bridegroom (Jesus) is getting the Bride (the church) ready to present to His Father.

He said we were to be a glorious church, without spot or wrinkle...holy and without blemish. (Eph. 5:27) Could anything be more exciting?

How do I know this is happening? There are a number of signs.

First of all, the gospel message is literally covering the earth, thanks to our modern communication systems, and people are responding.

Secondly, the "God is dead" era has had its day. The backlash it created has sent people scrambling for better answers... even the existence of God!

Next, old hates are being resolved and old wounds are being healed. When we see people, whose forefathers believed in slavery, apologizing to the descendants of those who suffered that shame, we know Jesus is washing out the spots and pressing out the wrinkles that have marred our "wedding garments" for too long. The next sign I see is the "rising up" of the men. When men pack into football stadiums by the thousand, not to see a game, but to learn how to become responsible men of God, we know there is a brand new "move" happening in our time. Blemishes are being removed.

Finally, our young people are on the move with "Jesus Marches" and "Jesus Rallies." When we see them handing out "What Would Jesus Do?" bracelets, we know God is preparing the generation that will usher in the Kingdom of God on earth.

I am not, in any way, denying the darkness that covers the earth. There will always be darkness, but it is in the night sky that the stars shine in all their brilliance. I believe that soon... very soon...the darkness will give way to a dawning we have never seen before and the stars will merge with the greater light.

At times, I imagine I hear the great "Wedding March" pealing through the heavens, and Jesus calling, "Come my Beloved, all things are ready. Don't Miss out!"

—M.L.A.

ABOUT THE AUTHOR

Merle Alexander was born, Merle Throckmorton, on May 21, 1921, in Prosser, Washington. The family moved to Port Angeles, Washington on the Olympic Peninsula in 1929. It was like moving to a different planet. The sharp contrast between the dry brown desert of eastern Washington and the towering rain forests of the Peninsula became a metaphor of her life.

The poverty of the Great Depression was the desert. The rain forest was the period of affluence that followed World War II. There were other contrasts. The life of a single career woman bore little resemblance to the full-time career of wife, mother, homemaker.

The greatest contrast of all was life before and after Jesus. The "before" was the desert. Life was going nowhere. Then, in mid-teen age, the brother nearest and dearest to her was killed in a tragic accident, and in the wake of that incident, "Jesus made Himself visible and healed my aching heart. The disappointments and hurts I had experienced were wiped away in an instant. All things became new."

Like most teenagers, Merle had no sense of direction for life after high school. All she cared about was getting through. Now, she was almost consumed with a passion for winning souls. To fulfill this calling, she entered the Salvation Army Officer's Training College in San Francisco and was commissioned in 1942.

After five years of Salvation Army officership, the Lord began to move in new directions in her life. "His agenda for me was more varied than I had ever thought possible. It included continuing education, an itinerant evangelistic ministry, and writing. But at the heart of it all was the ministry of intercessory prayer. Everything else came out of that. To me, it is the life of high privilege."

"God, You Are Incredible!" is her first book.